UNHEALTHY BEHAVIOR,
ABUSE AND ADDICTION COME FROM...

A PAIN IN THE GUT

PREVENTION, RECOVERY AND RENEWAL COME FROM
"APPROPRIATE LOVE"

Joseph C. Way, BA, BD, MDiv

ISBN 978-1-959071-86-0 (paperback)
ISBN 978-1-959071-87-7 (digital)

Printed in the United States of America

CONTENTS

DEDICATION

To my wife, Ruth, who is an example of appropriate love:
if not perfectly, then primarily; if not constantly, then
normally; and if not for everyone, then certainly for me.

PREFACE

Most of us have felt "a pain in the gut" that had no connection to any digestive disorder. We consciously and subconsciously spend a large amount of time and effort responding to that pain, either trying to get rid of it or to prevent its return. Such pain is a natural part of the human condition but without our conscientious care and caution it destroys us. When abundant and persistent, it prevents full development of the human potential and robs us of our

health and happiness. The degree of that pain's presence strongly indicates who we are and how we act.

I have been a clergyman, counselor, and therapist for more than forty years. During that time, I witnessed the debilitating effect of that pain in thousands of people who shared with me the excruciating pain in their guts. They helped me become acutely aware of its universal presence and its devastating results. In response to their needs, and mine, I deliberately sought acceptable ways to reduce its agony, eliminate its destructive presence and prevent its causes. This book prescribes a process and procedures designed to move us in that

direction. I call that movement "Renewal" or "Recovery."

The material in this book offers meaningful models for the renewal journey and tries to paint a big picture that enables us to

better identify where we are on life's road. It tells why we hurt, where relief is available, and how to avoid the pain. I have provided specific models, questions, examples, suggestions and insights to facilitate

that discovery and help us choose our response to what we see in the big picture. For those who desire and choose renewal, the suggestions may need personal adjustments or additions but the basic principle must not be altered or lost.

Much of this material was originally designed for persons in drug and alcohol treatment programs. I quickly recognized its application for any and all who need renewal. A pain in the gut makes renewal necessary. That pain in the gut comes from numerous sources and from abuse of many things.

Much of this material was first designed for the players who I thought were only traditional abusers and addicts. I later learned the players are almost everyone! Even if we never abused drugs and alcohol, we often have a very serious pain in our gut caused by some other malady. Therefore, the original setting and origin of the ideas need not prevent an open-minded examination or a broader application of them.

Initially, I made the normal and naive assumption that heavy abusers and addicts were distinctively different from the rest of us. Long ago, I learned the fallacy of that assumption. Their primary problem, like most of ours, is directly related to a pain in the gut. That false assumption is detrimental to our offer of aid and to their

attempt at recovery. We reason, "If they are different, why should we offer help and what good will it be?" They assume, "If I am different, as they say, and act, then I have justification for my behavior."

These attitudes prevent recovery and illustrate the necessity for a new approach to renewal. Heavy abusers and addicts are different from the rest of us only in degree, not kind. Almost without exception, each of us is addicted to something, abuses something, or acts in some way that tends to damage others and ourselves. Some of us are addicted to having our own way at any cost, to seeing only the negative in every situation and person, to a strict and daily routine, to one method for solving any problem, to social customs and family traditions, etc.

Our unrecognized maladies, personality disorders, habits, etc. may have a hold on us and may be as disruptive and demanding on us as addiction and abuse are for those whom we consider "different." Therefore, I deliberately use "abuse" and "addiction" in their broadest sense throughout this book and each is applicable far beyond the subjects of drugs and alcohol. They are often used in that connection but must not be mistakenly limited to those items. They speak of a lifestyle and are inclusive terms for certain kinds of habitual behavior.

Both reflect behavior as well as a specific state in which we may find ourselves.

There are often logical reasons for our irrational behavior! All levels of abuse, addiction, etc., are apparently the normal outcome of certain conditions and circumstances. Most frequently, all abuse is connected in some way to a pain in the gut. Recognition of that fact was a revelatory moment for me and forced me to seriously reconsider the causes and "cures" for all abuse. In response to that recognition, I began my search for a new recovery process and a more effective "cure" because most of the old approach made no sense.

This book reflects my search to uncover possible causes and to propose viable treatments for abuse and addiction at all levels and degrees. The book emphasizes what we all know, i.e., a cure is more effective when applied as a preventive measure before the malady develops. Renewal and prevention are made possible by the same identical thing, from having received healthy and wholesome love.

Words are imperfect vehicles for communicating ideas, so I offer an explanation for a few words that may first appear somewhat technical. Occasionally, they are but most often they are used in the broadest possible sense. I chose them because no other words communicated as well. They are inclusive, descriptive, polite, and easy- to- use shorthand words for big ideas. "Patient" and "client" are such words. Like "recovery" and "renewal" or "abuse" and "addiction," they are inclusive words that are not restricted to a formalized treatment setting or program. They always include everyone who hurts and who seeks renewal from any available source. "Patients" and "clients" often receive help from a "therapist" but the "therapist" is anyone who facilitates recovery, whether professionally trained or only a competent friend.

Much of my insight, information, and conclusions came from conversations with and observations of countless clients in diverse settings and situations. I am especially indebted to thousands of persons whom I met while they were in a treatment program. Many who came to me for help taught me things I never expected to learn. Drawing upon what I knew, what I learned from many sources, and what they taught me, I trust I gave them new insights in return. As we struggled together, I was able to make some sense out of what previously had been a senseless situation. I trust the pain and agony of our travels will make the journey of others less painful and more productive. If this book can facilitate that kind of journey, their efforts and mine were not in vain. I sincerely hope this book presents meaningful models for anyone who seeks renewal. I trust it will help us eliminate and prevent "a pain in the gut."

Three people deserve special thanks for their invaluable help toward the completion of this book. My wife served as a sounding board, research assistant, and overall evaluator. Our son, a college professor,skillfully identified misspelled words, improper verbs and pronouns,fuzzy phrases, and faulty punctuation. He also graciously granted permission to use his superb poem found at the end of chapter nine, entitled "Fledgling." Our daughter used her artistic skills to help design a suggested cover for the book.

CHAPTER 1

A Man Without a Model

I never planned to work as a counselor and therapist with alcoholor drug abusers. My plans abruptly changed when the Air Force assigned me to a base as one of twenty-five chaplains on the staff.That very large chapel section was divided into specific work areas. The ranking chaplain in each area served as the supervisor and reported to the base senior chaplain, the administrative head of thetotal chapel program.

At a regular weekly meeting, the senior chaplain asked his staff for a volunteer to lecture top-ranking officers and enlisted personnel who desperately needed assistance when they counseled with subordinates who had alcohol or drug problems. No one volunteered. The senior base chaplain instructed my supervisor either deliver the lecture or assign it to another. During our staff meeting, my supervisor asked for a volunteer. Once again, no one accepted.

Taking a page from the senior chaplain's book, he turned to me and said, "Will you give it?" As a person who always tried to do what the boss requested, I agreed to give the lecture. Little did I suspect the impact that assignment would have on my life.

Following days of agonizing thought and effort, I reported to the designated place for the lecture and began the presentation. I speak with greater ease and clarity when I have a chalkboard nearby and a piece of chalk in my hand. During the presentation, I wrote selected words on the chalkboard, drew circles and squares, and emphasized points with arrows and stars.

The alert group responded well and, during the presentation, the audience had an opportunity to raise questions and make comments. In response to each, I frequently recorded information on the chalkboard and emphasized points with arrows, circles, etc. During one lively exchange, while my back was to the audience as I wrote on the chalkboard, someone made a comment.

Without looking back or knowing who had spoken, I quickly and politely replied, "I don't believe you realize the ramifications of what you are saying," and kept on writing and talking as I emphasized my point.

After a short time, everyone seemed to agree the comment from the audience did not support the idea under discussion and should be dismissed. Momentarily, someone in the audience spoke and I recognized it came from the person I previously corrected. Wishing to identify the person, I moved so that I could clearly see him, an action that may have been a mistake!

I was shocked to discover the voice belonged to a two-star General. He was the commander of the largest training base in the Air Force and the man who had initially directed a chaplain present the lecture. Needless to say, I suffered a slight panic attack when I realized what had just transpired. It dawned on me that I had made it beyond the incident and had no need or excuse to stop. I plowed ahead with the presentation and received positive responses from the participants.

After the lecture, I further pondered what had happened with the General. That night I informed my wife what I did and that I could be in trouble. I told no other person about the event. The following morning, I went to work with some apprehension. Shortly after reaching my office, I received a phone call from the senior base chaplain. My heart raced because he seldom called our section that early in the day and even more seldom did he talk to me by phone.

In a loud voice, he asked, "What did you do at that lecture yesterday?"

My legs grew weak. I replied, "I tried to tell them the truth." He said, "The General just called me."

I slid further down in my chair.

Then he added, "The General was very impressed with what you said and did. He wants you assigned to the Base Rehabilitation Team that counsels and works with our military personnel who have problems with alcohol or drug abuse."

I suspect there was sweat on my brow and a weird smile on my face after hearing that. You can be sure this story would not be told if it were vastly different.

Many times, since I thought about that experience and all the experiences that followed, perhaps all because I told a General, he didn't know what he was saying. That General may have laughed last because no one really wanted an assignment to the rehabilitation team. It was such grueling work and often with people who had little desire to overcome their problems.

To this day, I don't know if that General truly appreciated what I said and did during that lecture or if he got really mad and punished me with the assignment. Regardless of why I was assigned to that rehabilitation team, reward or punishment, I was there. I determined to do what I could to help those who wanted help, as well as do what I could for those who did not initially want it. Having made that decision, I truly became a man without a model to follow.

My involvement in the recovery process and my endeavor to become educated about abuse, addiction and recovery began by way of the back door. I had no intention to enter but I am happy I did. In the many years that followed, through many hours of serious study and learning from thousands of abusers, I gathered insights I feel compelled to share.

One reason for sharing them is due to what several serious abusers said to me. On more than one occasion, someone asked if I am a recovering addict. When I answered in the negative, more than one person doubted my answer because they said, "You can't understand what it's like to be an abuser, as you obviously do unless you are one."

I took that as the highest compliment anyone could give me. I accepted their comments as a validation of my insight into their problems and my ability to help them. At that point in time, I certainly did not consider myself an abuser, having never touched alcohol or illegal drugs. Even though I had significant insight into their problems, I did not recognize my tendency to also abuse something or someone. Neither they nor I recognized how similar we were. Perhaps they knew better than I.

While many of those who made that statement lacked formal education, apparently, they knew more than I realized. I now believe I understood them because I had some understanding of myself and the human condition. I subconsciously connected with them because, in some sense and to some degree, I have been where they were but had not made the connection between their abuse and mine.

Eventually, I recognized the validity of their statement because abuse and addiction extend far beyond drugs and alcohol. I understood and empathized with them because I also tend to abuse and must constantly fight against the tendency. I empathized with their struggle because it is also my struggle and the struggle of every person. Though hidden beyond my conscious awareness, I sensed that I could help because I am also engaged in a somewhat similar battle in which I made some progress. Their struggle was my struggle.

I don't know at what point in my learning process I concluded that all of us are addicted to something, or bordering on it. Having reached that point, I first endeavored to learn about myself and then all humanity. I wanted not only to learn what frequently leads to abuse and addiction but also to learn what made each of us who we are. I looked for ways to overcome abuse and addiction of every kind and degree, even that which often goes by some other name.

Since prevention is much better than a cure, I sought insights that might be useful at each end of the spectrum. To effectively facilitate recovery and renewal, to help remove the pain in their gut, I must first better understand my pain and find personal renewal. I needed an effective model to guide me as I sought to guide others.

Since prevention is much better than a cure, I sought insights that might be useful at each end of the spectrum. To effectively facilitate recovery and renewal, to help remove the pain in their gut, I must first better understand my pain and find personal renewal. I needed an effective model to guide me as I sought to guide others.

Since the day that General thrust me into a situation for which I felt ill-prepared, I developed several models and ideas designed to facilitate the recovery and renewal process. Apparently, our problems originate with a pain in the gut, not the head. If that is true, then recovery and prevention must begin by reducing the pain. Likewise, I have developed ideas that may help prevent pain, abuse and addiction of all degrees and types. I initially formulated ideals and insights that helped me.

Since many clients and patients enthusiastically received them, they may be helpful to others. I trust these shared insights will stimulate others to find a meaningful model that prevents painful maladies and provides renewal. May that be true for those who desire renewal and for those who help others in their search for it. I can safely say I am no longer a man without a model.

CHAPTER 2

Making a Model

Military assignments provided many unexpected experiences for me. None provided more unexpected opportunities than the one that positioned me as a counselor and therapist for drug and alcohol rehabilitation. Having been abruptly assigned to that position without warning, I recognized how little I knew about abuse, addiction and recovery. Having a deep desire to learn, I began a quest for knowledge that continues this day.

During that quest, I formulated and repeatedly reformulated ideas, models, and paradigms that helped me get a mental picture of abusers, addiction, the healing process and preventive measures. My creative struggle began with two basic assumptions. First, our comprehension of an idea will be greatly enhanced when we not only hear it expressed but also see it in a picture or model. Second, having intellectually grasped the idea to some degree, we are more likely to make a personal application of it when we see ourselves in the picture. It is also possible that seeing ourselves in the picture may help us better understand the idea.

These two assumptions became guiding principles in my search for some way to help those adversely affected by a pain in the gut. My search began with those who abused alcohol but I later discovered an application to other issues.

I developed a skeleton for the following model many years ago but I refined it more than once. The model begins with circle number one, labeled "Subject." There is no particular meaning or magic in using a circle. Squares, triangles, or dots will do. Perhaps the reason I use circles is that if I go around in circles long enough, I might become a big wheel.

1

The "Subject" is precisely what the word implies, the topic under consideration. It may be whatever the human mind can comprehend, from an awareness of one's own existence to any simple, complex, or remote idea. From various sources, the identity of which is not important at this juncture, the "Subject" comes into existence in one's mind. With the passing of time, the person who harbors the subject in their mind realizes there is something significant beyond and apart from the subject that has some bearing or influence upon understanding and responding to the subject. That awareness may not necessarily be conscious but one has a real sense that it is there and that it has something to do with the subject. In fact, an isolated subject cannot be fully understood.

Therefore, one's understanding of it depends, in some measure, upon the existence of something beyond it. That "something" beyond the "Subject," which helps to understand it, is the "Significant."

The next step in making this model requires a second circle on the same level as the first with some space between the two circles. Circle number two is labeled "Significant." To indicate the passing of time, draw a line between the two circles. Since there is an interaction between the "Subject" and the "Significant," place an arrow point on each end of the line.

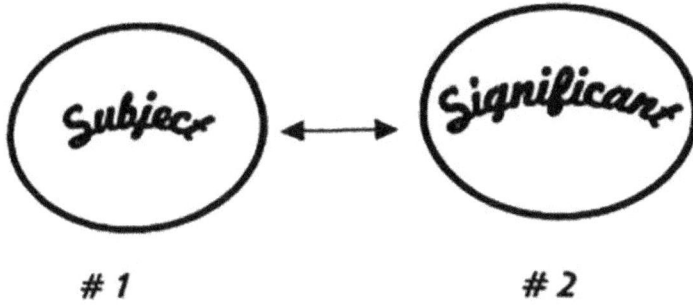

#1   #2

An illustration is in order. Let us use "automobile" as the "Subject." What are we talking about? Upon close scrutiny, "automobile" tells little about what one has in mind. Since an automobile is a self-propelled vehicle, without further information you would have a hard time locating a particular car in the parking lot. By definition, you know it is not a bicycle, red wagon, or roller skate. That is very important. The subject, automobile, is acted upon, enlarged by something beyond it. The material contained in the "Significant" circle serves that precise purpose.

The second circle contains such items as make, model, style, color, number of doors or wheels, etc. They provide handles that enable us to intellectually grasp "automobile." Now, if I say my automobile is a 1980 Datsun, five-speed, blue, two-door hatchback, most anyone can go to the parking lot and find it.

Additional and specific information enables a stranger to find my automobile. If there are no known factors acting upon the subject, one has a tough time understanding the full meaning of "automobile." When the "Significant" circle holds abundant content, the "Subject" comes into sharper focus. I believe this holds true for any subject one may suggest, be it "house," "job," "person," etc.

Several points about the "Subject" and the "Significant" require special attention. The "Subject" is always singular, or at least a single item, issue or idea. The "Significant," almost without fail, is multiple or contains more than one issue or item. The more awareness we have of the numerous items contained in the "Significant" that relate to and act upon the "Subject" the clearer the "Subject" becomes.

Our awareness of what is significant, or lack thereof, is extremely crucial. That awareness does not automatically come to us on the basis of our humanity nor does it come to us at a certain age, stage, or position in life. There is no guarantee that it will come to anyone. However, the fact that we are functioning individuals indicates the process is operative at some level.

The "Significant" represents the mind's awareness of factors or things that affect the "Subject" and perhaps the person who has the "Subject" in mind. The "Significant" can be whatever the human mind comprehends as being apart from and affecting the "Subject" at that moment. Anything that affects the "Subject" is "Significant" but many of those things are frequently beyond our awareness. By nature, design and accident we discover the "Significant" for ourselves, and maybe for others. Theories of human growth and development illustrate the natural process of this discovery.

Since awareness of what is "Significant" is so important, we must consider its sources. The sources may be different for different people but I suspect they are surprisingly similar. Our conviction of what is significant comes from several places quite common to all. The initial source is usually our parents who, long before we were aware of what they were doing, were steadily and persistently telling us what was significant for specific subjects.

Someone reported a conversation between my father-in-law and his son during which they discussed politics. "I will never tell you for whom to vote," my father-in-law said. "I want you to always vote for the right man, but remember, the right man will always be running on the Democratic ticket."

I fondly remember purchasing my first car. My father and I never discussed the kind of car I should buy. He had owned Fords all my life. My first and only stop was at the Ford dealership, the one at which he repeatedly traded. I gave no serious consideration to buying a Chevrolet or Dodge. My father never said, "Always buy a Ford." He didn't have to say it. He demonstrated it and I understood it, without even knowing that I understood!

Some parents make conscious and extensive effort to determine what their child considers significant when thinking about a specific subject. Other parents just do it without trying. Throughout our childhood, our parents indicated by words and actions what was really significant to them in dealing with numerous and specific subjects. Even if they knew what they were doing, we did not, and they didn't tell us what was going on. Some of us were fortunate to have parents with whom we could openly discuss what was or was not significant and we are much the wiser for it.

Being social creatures, we also gather information on what is significant for certain subjects from our peers. For that reason alone, "recess" is one of the most important classes at school, especially when it unexpectedly broadens the mind of the lesser informed. During our association with others, we learn what they consider significant, much of which probably came directly from their parents. What they and their parents think is seldom identical to what we and our parents think. The degree of difference helps to determine new possibilities that may be significant to a subject. Even though that difference may be or become the source of great pain, it is perhaps the most fertile field for expanding our awareness of the "Significant."

As obvious from the above, personal experience helps us sort out what is significant. This personal sorting process is both conscious and subconscious, lasting from the cradle to the grave, for most of us. Our young son, about eighteen months old, painfully illustrated the learning process through personal experience.

We lived in an old house heated by one coal or wood-burning heater that sat away from the wall in the dining room. Our son was in the room with the heater and I was in the adjacent living room. The heater had a fire in it. He looked at me, pointed toward the heater, and walked toward it saying, "Hot, hot, hot." I asked him to stop but he kept walking with a finger out front. Before I reached him, he reached the heater. Instantly, a big blister appeared on his finger and tears came to his eyes. From that day, he never needed to touch an active heater to discover the meaning of "hot."

His experience, like many of our own, provided of meaningful messages about what is significant. We most often carry those messages wherever we go. However, under certain conditions and circumstances, we tend to forget or disregard what we learned. What we learned may later prove to be inaccurate or incomplete. We usually learn that through personal experience!

Personal experience is our greatest teacher. Perhaps, we could make the argument that it is our only true teacher. Either way, learning is frequently influenced by numerous items beyond our control or recognition. Because of our nature, each person's various experiences convince them certain things are extremely significant, even when dealing with diverse subjects.

Professors and teachers enable us to increase our awareness of what is significant for certain subjects. Otherwise, what is their purpose? They epitomize the educational process that, I believe, mirrors the principle I seek to explain here. We are well aware that professors can only do so much for our learning process. They say what they see as significant but we must appropriate it and make it our own. At least in their area of expertise, their pool of awareness is normally greater than the pupil's pool. They share their abundance and offer us an opportunity to expand our personal knowledge.

Pastors, priests, and rabbis provide special input in terms of what is significant to specific subjects. For centuries, these persons have made a unique contribution to and had special influence on the development of our thought process. They are the respected religious authority and their word is law for those who view them as one step below God. Religious authority is so important to so many. Therefore, those who speak authoritatively in its behalf wield enormous influence.

Most of what was previously said about parents, peers, and professors can also be truthfully said about them. More must be said because they have been held in exceptionally high esteem, thereby giving them special influence. Like parents, peers, professors and possibly personal experiences, some of their contributions have resulted in immeasurable good while others may have produced more detriment than good. In fairness to everyone, it is not they who deserve full credit for either. Without doubt, they exert pronounced, unquestioned and permanent influence on what many of us believe significant.

There are other possible sources from which we assimilate our own ideas of things significant to a subject but we need not pursue them. However, it is extremely crucial to emphasize the importance of what one adds or does not add from all sources. It takes no stretch of our imagination to recognize the radical difference that may exist between similar or separate sources.

Compare the input from a well-educated parent with one who quit school in the eighth grade. This is not meant to denigrate those with lesser education nor is it meant to bestow sainthood on those who possess advanced degrees. We usually assume higher education results in a greater awareness level, at least in some areas.

Consider also the personal experiences of a wanted child born into the lap of luxury with ideal parents possessing advanced degrees and high social status. Compare that child with one who lives in the slums with an unwed mother on welfare. Which of these children will more likely have the advantage from outside sources that make a broader positive contribution to their awareness of what is significant? The issue here is not the worth of a child but rather the availability of substantial and positive inputs to a child's awareness. We all know that for every child there is, and always will be, a radical difference between parents, peers, personal experiences, professors and pastors. That is just the way our world is. Remember also that all those differences are not necessarily negative. Loving, honest, poor and uneducated parents may teach a child the fundamentals for a meaningful life that would not have been taught by the rich and famous. Valuable contributions are not limited to the formally educated and socially privileged. However, the odds are in their favor.

I recall my childhood in rural Mississippi to illustrate my point. Neither my father nor mother went beyond the eighth grade in public school but my father was my wisest teacher about life. There were ten students in my high school graduating class, nine boys and one girl. The teachers were often recent college graduates, if they had even finished, or else aged settlers whose passion for teaching had waned.

From that small rural high school, I went to Millsaps College in Jackson, Mississippi, which carried a high national scholastic ranking. The first step in my additional education was the realization of how little information I knew compared to those who graduated from outstanding high schools in the state. Many of my fellow students also had more material possessions and less financial worries, yet several of those students sought my help to find meaning in their life.

Most of us agree that greater advantages are likely available to a healthy child of energetic, affluent, and educated parents. Conversely, the child of poor, uneducated, lethargic, and unemployed parents will most often lack some advantages others have. However, we have no guarantee it always happens this way. The situation and conditions into which we are born or exist will greatly affect what we believe to be significant about certain subjects. Having consciously or subconsciously drawn some conclusion about what is significant for a specific subject, we will be guided by it until it is changed. If, and when, change comes, it will come only after something new enters the "Significant" circle.

Let us now move to the next step of our model. Midway between circles one and two, and somewhat higher than they, place a third circle and label it "Supreme." As between circles one and two, draw a line between circles two and three. This line also indicates passing of time. Items in the "Significant" act upon the "Supreme." There is interaction between the two. Place an arrow point on each of the line to indicate interaction

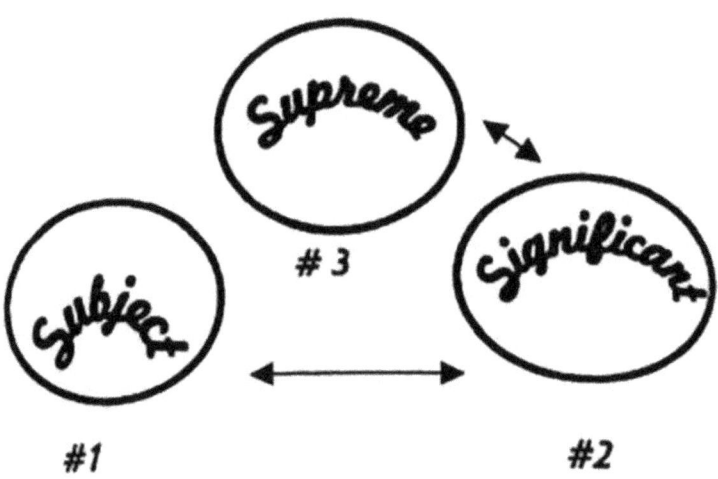

I cannot prove what happens at this juncture but I am fully convinced the process always transpires. As the mind evaluates certain ideas, objects, persons, etc., considers "Significant" for a "Subject," I contend that most often, if not always, and subconsciously, if not consciously, a unique action occurs. As we contemplate a subject, any subject, our mind sorts through all or selected items contained in the "Significant" for that specific "Subject."

For some reason that may or may not be discernible, the mind elevates from the "Significant" one single factor as most important while dealing with that "Subject" at that moment. The position of circle three in the diagram illustrates the elevating process and we label it "Supreme" because it contains what we consider most important to the "Subject." Our "Supreme" dictates, controls, all our behavior in reference to that "Subject" at that time. Every "Supreme" is drawn from the "Significant." Every item in the "Significant" for that "Subject" has the potential to become the "Supreme."

When the "Subject" changes, there will almost always be some major or minor change in the "Significant" and there may or may not be a change in what becomes "Supreme." It is very important to note that we restrict the items eventually elevated to the "Supreme," consequently causing repetition. Even with different "Subjects," the same "Supreme" may surface, thereby indicating its controlling influence on our life. The degree of repetition in the "Supreme" is extremely indicative of a major commitment and lifestyle. The more prominent and repetitious the "Supreme," the greater influence it has on a person's values and behavior.

Eventually and without fail, we consciously or subconsciously select one "Supreme" that is most important in our life. Otherwise, we are in serious trouble. The unwillingness or inability to consciously select a "Supreme" for our life may be the key to understanding certain human behavior. Life has no meaning or purpose without its "god" and likely will not last long or will be extremely chaotic. The primary trouble usually comes not from a lack of choice but because we choose unwisely or unintentionally.

Whatever "Supreme" we select for our life becomes our "god," which is the meaning of "Supreme" in this connection. Our "god" controls our response to our ultimate concern or a lesser one, just as the selected "Supreme" for any "Subject" controls our action in reference to it. Our over-arching and life directing "Supreme," our "god," may be alcohol, drugs, sex, cigarettes, coffee, sweets, a good feeling, God, etc. The list of possibilities is almost endless. We are likely addicted to one of these numerous possibilities. Realization of that fact may shock some of us but it might also open a door to freedom for others.

Hopefully, all of the above will become cleared when we complete our intended model. It only adds a pictorial presentation of what has been given in words. To complete the model, draw a line between circles three and one to indicated passing of time. Place an arrow point at each end of the line to also indicated interaction between the content in the circles. Interactions between the two and the powerful control of the "Supreme" over the "Subject" were indicated above. In every situation, the "Supreme" for any "Subject" at a given moment dictates our behavior in reference to that "Subject." The completed model reflects the decision making process and its final outcome.

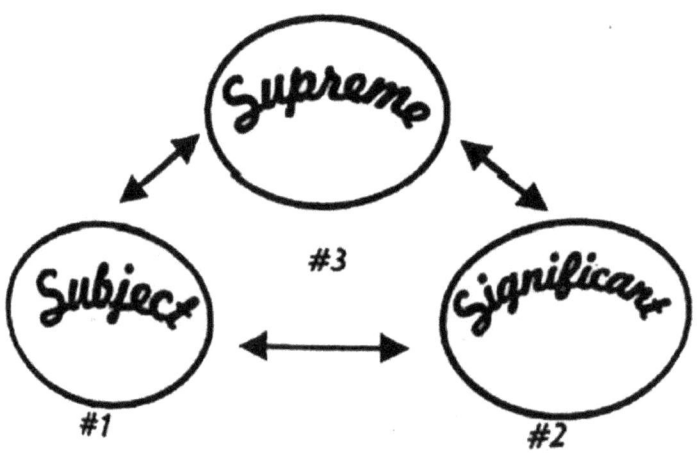

Perhaps the meaning of this model will become more apparent if we return to the earlier illustration about automobiles. Suppose we decide to purchase one. What will we buy? Apply the model described above and the answer is quite obvious. The "Subject" is "purchasing an automobile." The "Significant" includes such things as make, model, color, price, style, etc.

One specific thing will determine what automobile we buy, which is our "Supreme" concern. If we elevate color as the determining factor and want a yellow car, we will not buy a red one.

If our supreme concern is a yellow car, we will pass up a great bargain on a green one. If for some reason we are convinced we must drive a Ford, no one will ever persuade us to drive a Chevrolet.

If we have only five hundred dollars to spend, and that is our supreme concern, we will likely buy the first car offered for five hundred dollars, regardless of its color. If we must have a car to meet some other supreme concern, we will buy something that meets that need. Other significant items do not totally disappear and often figure in the decision but they always take a back seat to the supreme concern.

We may change the "Subject" and renew the process. I frequently asked clients and patients to identify the reason for their abusive behavior. Their answers included boredom, peer pressure, personal problems of all sorts, escape from reality, etc. Each of their proposed reasons can be inserted into the model as "Subject." Those persons readily admitted significant factors led them to their present state. They also admitted there were several things they could have done in response to their condition and the feelings it generated.

Almost without exception, alcohol, drugs and other abusive practices were among several things that enabled them to deal with the feelings associated with the identified subject. At the point they began to depend upon alcohol, drugs, etc. as the primary way to deal with that "Subject," they were in deep trouble. At that point, they were heavy abusers or addicted. Alcohol, drugs or abusive behavior became their "Supreme" when dealing with the "Subject." Most frequently, the "Subject" is best understood as a feeling. The same is true for addiction to food, sex, cigarettes, etc.

For an additional illustration, we consider a very shy person. Shyness, or the unpleasant feeling it creates, is our "Subject." There are many ways of responding to the feeling it generates, both positively and negatively. If a person eventually chooses alcohol as the "Supreme" response to the feeling, the person will most likely self-medicate by drinking when the feeling occurs or to prevent its occurrence. Anything once chosen from various possibilities to tentatively eliminate an unwanted feeling may become an almost automatic response in dealing with that feeling. When no other options are considered, when the response becomes automatic, for this or any "Subject" we name, addiction has occurred.

Addiction of any sort primarily bypasses the "Significant" circle in the diagram for that "Subject." When a certain "Subject" arises, addicted persons skip over the prioritizing and sorting process and automatically jump to the previous "Supreme" for guidance in their response to that matter. That process inactivates the second circle of our model and indicates unhealthy behavior.

Additional examples and illustrations of the model's use are readily available. It is only necessary to change the verbiage. For every subject there is a model and the model apparently is applicable to every conceivable subject. We enhance the model's value with additional illustrations of its encompassing scope.

We select a person's "career" as a "Subject." Significant factors in one's career include professionalism, performance, and promotion. Our behavior is largely determined by choosing a supreme concern. If I choose professionalism as my "Supreme." I will concentrate on appearance, being knowledgeable, being courteous, doing my assigned job expeditiously and correctly, etc. If I choose performance, my main concern is getting the job accomplished at any and all cost. I will come early and remain late while sacrificing other things for my family and myself. The job drives my behavior.

If I choose promotion, I will do whatever it takes to advance my position and pay, with little or no regard for how professional I may be or when and how a particular job gets done. I will renounce other stated values if doing so enhances promotion possibilities. The last point was perfectly illustrated by an Air Force chaplain supervisor who told me he wished he was a non-drinker like me but he would drink anything if he thought it would help him get promoted. Having first chosen what is most important to us, certain behavior is basically inevitable.

Our action will always be affected by whatever we choose as "Supreme." If you want to know what any one considers important, observe what they do and you will get a strong clue. The old timers in rural Mississippi said, "You can tell a man's religion by the way he treats his mule." Their words contain great wisdom and they speak precisely to our point. Those unsophisticated farmers did not recognize the ramifications of their words but they discovered a profound truth. Just for the record, they did not learn that truth from a college professor but from personal experience. The way I treat my mule, my wife, my neighbor, myself, etc. proclaims what is truly important to me. We cannot fool others or ourselves for very long.

This model provides a key for understanding many things. It depicts the natural process of human growth and development, or the lack of it. Knowing the information contained in any personal model helps us better understand why that person acts as they do. Little or very limited information contained in a personal model indicates illness, immaturity, ignorance or some combination of all three. To see and understand my personal model is to see and understand myself. For me to see and understand your model is to understand you.

In light of this model, interpersonal conflicts are both anticipated and identified. If two people are to experience complete harmony on any subject, their personal models for that subject must basically agree, especially for the "Supreme" concern. Suppose a mother encouraged her daughter to exercise caution when selecting a mate. According to the mother, rich and educated men make better mates. What is most likely to happen when the daughter, eighteen years of age, informs her mother that she is going to marry a twenty-eight-year-old high school dropout who has a prison record and is presently pumping gas at the local service station? Love is the foremost concern for the daughter but her mother is sure other things are more important. Our model predicts what will follow the announcement because the mother's "Supreme" is vastly different from the daughters on the subject of marriage. Congruent and matching models predict greater agreement and incongruent models almost always indicate future problems with another person. Other illustrations are numerous.

Consider a couple who loves animals and each willingly sacrifices other enjoyable things in order to keep a horse. Ponder a family in which the father is offered a huge promotion if they move to a large and distant city but the family unanimously decides to remain where they are. These families have harmony because they have matching models.

What about a person who loves to stay up all night and sleep all day but rooms with someone who keeps the same hours as chickens? What about being married to a miserly mate but you believe money was made to spend immediately and frivolously? Problems are guaranteed for them because their models do not match. We avoid serious conflicts with others by having an identical "Supreme." Incongruent models inevitably encourage conflict. It can be no other way.

This model is quite useful in understanding intrapersonal conflicts. Much that was said about interpersonal conflicts is applicable to intrapersonal conflicts. A person's inner tranquility and delightful demeanor depend on congruent personal models for different subjects. Each mind contains as many models as individual "Subjects," with some models more developed than others. The "Supreme" for one "Subject" must harmonize with the "Supreme" for another "Subject" or personal conflict ensues. Every lesser "Supreme" must pleasantly fit under the umbrella of our ultimate "Supreme" or a person is "a house divided against itself." The conflict causes pain and is most often reflected in behavior.

A "divided self" and the inability or unwillingness to formulate congruent models are the undercurrents that often lead to addiction, abuse, deviant behavior, and human misery. We move toward recovery and renewal by purposefully choosing an ultimate "Supreme." Next, we must synchronize the "Supreme" for each individual model with our ultimate concern and with each secondary "Supreme." Our ultimate "Supreme" unifies our life, giving it direction and purpose. If wisely chosen, it has the power to lead us toward wholeness. If unwisely or unintentionally chosen, it tends to destroy us. The two disciplines of Psychology and Judeo-Christian religion have tried to tell us that for years. Perhaps we should take them seriously.

Even though imperfect, this model helps us better understand human behavior. It is simple enough to easily understand but unique enough to inform and refresh. It portrays in pictorial form the process through which we go to select what is important to us. It indicates how we reached our present position, points to why we confront certain difficulties and suggests how we may change our behavior and our life. It offers clues to discover the root of many personal problems. It also provides preventive measures and possible cures for others. Hopefully, it enables us to see and understand where we are in life's big picture. If it can do that for us, it will then offer renewal by providing a model to remove at least some of the pain from our gut.

CHAPTER 3

Mending Our Model

If the previous model depicts and partially describes abuse and addiction, it declares how and where recovery begins. It also suggests possibilities for preventing debilitating pain in our gut. Abusers and addicts at every level apparently reflect a broken model that must be mended before we can experience a meaningful and healthy existence. A broken or deformed personal model must be mended, perhaps radically renovated, if recovery and renewal are to occur. If much of our model is wrecked, we may never recover without competent outside help, depending on how severe the damage. Properly mending a personal model and recovery will be an identical process in most cases.

Repair and recovery properly begin at the point of our pain. Many people are well aware of what is causing their immediate problems, i.e., use of drugs or alcohol, sexual abuse, over eating, etc. They also know the mess they made of themselves and with others. Deep within, most are unhappy with what happened to them and those for whom they care. Relief of personal pain is the primary reason they seek help. They are much more likely to respond favorably to available assistance if approached at the point of their pain, rather than at the point of family and finance. They usually know what we easily forget. Many of them realize they have some form of abuse or addiction, precipitated by pain, and they remain rather helpless until its stranglehold is broken. Those who offer help from any other perspective declare a lack of understanding for who and where both helper and patient are.

In terms of the above model, addiction obliterates the "Significant" for at least that "Subject" in a personal model. The extent of obliteration is likely related to the degree of pain, abuse or addiction. Recovery comes by restoring the person's awareness of what is "Significant" and allowing the entire model to function again for every "Subject."

Return to the prescribed model with "abuse" or "addiction" as the "Subject." Suffering persons desiring recovery must deal with their slavery to addiction or abuse. It now dominates much of their life. A person must be led carefully and repeatedly to discuss that fact and asked, "What do you want to do about it?" Two things are accomplished with this approach. It disallows denial by the person and affirms to them that the therapist is on target. The therapist's questions offer some open options for the patient. In terms of the model, the therapist encourages the patient to "mend" their guidelines for life. Patients are offered opportunities and experiences designed to restore an awareness of the "Significant" circle.

With time and proper assistance, the person will be able to consciously refill the "Significant" circle and deliberately choose a new "Supreme." Patients must learn new ways to appropriately deal with personal pain. Mending a model related to a specific pain, abuse and addiction normally requires remodeling for other subjects, thereby transforming much of the person's life.

This brief description of the mending process does not indicate the enormous task it likely will be. The ease with which it is described may be the exact opposite of its difficulty to accomplish. In fact, we never fully complete the process and it demands constant sustenance if it continues. Badly broken models may need professional help because successful recovery is definitely doubtful without it. In severe cases, the risk of failure is too great for anyone to attempt recovery alone. In less severe cases, we may be very successful without professional help but there is always a danger in trying to heal ourselves.

Mending the model is not only necessary for the addicted and the abuser but it may also be necessary for those who assist others on the recovery journey. Stated bluntly, the models for recovery used by many treatment centers, counselors, therapists and well-meaning friends need radical repair. Improvements may have been made since I last worked in a program. I waged a continuing battle with the directors of almost every program in which I served, primarily because they consistently sought to initiate recovery at an improper point. Much of what was said and done in those programs was very helpful if offered in a more appropriate sequence.

Almost without fail, the programs began with an attempt to connect intellectually with the patient. Patients were often reminded of their poor physical condition, their desperate financial straits, their shattered relationship with family and former friends, their present and possible future unemployment, etc. Perpetrators of such attempts never understood why many patients quit the program and had no clue to the high rate of immediate recidivism for graduates. Concerned friends and family members frequently made the same mistakes. They meant well but operated from an improper recovery model.

The suggested model offers some help in understanding such results. Programs addressed issues with which the patients could not deal because their supreme concern, their god, held them in its grip. They can never recover unless and until that grip is broken. Participation in such a program added to the existing frustrations in the patients, who long ago learned that drugs or drink would make those painful feelings go away for a little while. It is no wonder the patients wanted a drink! The program increased their pain.

Even under the stated attempt to help, formal rehab programs and suggestions from associates have at times made matters worse for participants by unknowingly encouraging the opposite of what was intended. When that is the case, that model must be mended in order to facilitate rehabilitation. We may substitute the name to any recovery effort or program by anyone and repeat what we have said. Recovery begins where the patient is, never where the therapist/ helper is or wants the patient to be. The personal agenda and model of the therapist/helper are crucial. If the patient is to be helped, the therapist/ helper must be conditioned to truly help the patient. That sounds strange but it is alarming how many therapists, counselors and well-meaning friends are in the business for reasons other than helping patients recover Many of them hold a hidden agenda of their own. Some have a personal problem or a family member who needs serious help so they are primarily searching for personal answers. I am deeply disturbed by the number of program directors who have little knowledge about or concern for the recovery process. It is something they do because their job description calls for it or it is a well-paying job. There are others who mean well but are misguided in their attempts to help. In fairness to all, some provide excellent assistance to those seeking recovery. Regardless of who or where they are, all ineffective would-be helpers need to mend their model.

An effective therapist quickly learns where the patient is and affirms the patient in that present position. Patients will readily reveal to a competent therapist where they are, especially if the therapist treats the patient with dignity and respect while carefully listening and gently probing. The patient may be sick but most of them are well enough to immediately discern if the therapist and treatment program are honestly offering help where they are.

The key to discernment is based on an increase or reduction of their personal pain. I suspect their discernment is initially at an unconscious level. When the patient decides the helper or treatment program is competent and trustworthy, the patient is prone to enter the mending process. Any other approach is doomed to failure.

Having been abruptly thrust into the role of counselor and therapist in a treatment program, I needed to mend my own model for helping. Contrary to what I had believed, most patients were intellectually sharp and were perhaps more so earlier in their life. The more association I had with them the more I realized the majority of them were advanced for the opportunities they had. They did or did not hold a degree from some major university but the majority of them held a degree from the "School of Hard Knocks." In earlier days, their advanced abilities sometimes set them apart. In some cases, that was the very thing that helped cause their problem. They knew more, saw more and felt more deeply than their associates.

There is a clue for why many were so adept at evaluating a counselor or treatment program. Many of them were repeatedly reminded by word and deed that they were different and then led to believe that was bad. If you doubt their amazing savvy, listen carefully to their story of survival before and after addiction. Hear them tell of a horrible home life and how they learned to cope with abusive and alcoholic parents. Hear them tell what they ate, how often, and how they got it. Picture them migrating with the seasons so they would be more comfortable while living in a lean-to made of brush or under a bridge.

Observe their extraordinary resourcefulness in getting a drink or fix when they really wanted it but had no money. Surviving life's threatening and painful experiences indicates their intellectual ability. Many of us would not survive similar ordeals. I marveled at their survival skills and often shared that fact with them. Having heard me validate them by that recognition, they often smiled, nodded and listened to whatever else I had to say.

My opinions about and approach to recovery were radically changed when I realized abuse does not occur because of what is or is not in our head but rather because of what is or is not in our "guts." Said differently, abuse is not from the intellectual level but rather from the emotional level. This is true for abuse at any level and degree. Since that is true, recovery must always begin within the emotions or feelings of the person. That is where their problem is and that is where recovery must begin. Otherwise, they never recover.

After hundreds of personal interviews with patients and numerous hours of searching records for any resemblance of a pattern, one thing emerged in almost every patient and especially in those who were addicted. The common thread that bound them was their description of themselves. Almost everyone had a firm impression that they were "no good" or inadequate, accompanied by an indescribable pain in their gut. They verbalized it in almost identical terms. The question, "How do you describe yourself" or "What do you think of yourself" was most frequently answered with, "I'm no damn good."

An alarmingly large number could identify the specific time, place, and event when they were fully convinced of it. Those who were less specific were just as sure of that gut feeling and could relate the approximate time and circumstances when they first felt it. One after another told of discovering how drugs, drink or some other abusive behavior would diminish that feeling or even make it disappears for a little while. Therefore, they did drugs, drank, ate excessively, abused others, etc. in order to get temporary relief. The implications of what they said finally dawned upon me. They "used" or "abused" primarily because they sought relief from the pain deep inside their gut. They became guilty of abuse, in whatever form, not because they enjoyed it but, in an effort, to find relief from their pain. "Feelings" are fundamental to understanding abuse, addiction and recovery. They deserve special attention, which they will receive at a later time.

The model presented in the previous chapter provides clues to better understand the process of recovery and renewal. Perhaps previous recovery efforts were less successful because too many of us were determined to use ineffective models. The condition of those who practice abuse and addiction verifies the need to mend their model in order for recovery and renewal to occur. The ineffectiveness of many counselors, therapists and helpers necessitates change so that they may more effectively help others mend their model for life. Since all of us are human, it may sometimes be necessary for each of us to mend our personal model in order to diminish or prevent a pain in our gut. At certain times, model mending may be wise and at other times it is a matter of life or death.

CHAPTER 4

The Seedbed of Abuse

Most, if not all, human actions are apparently motivated either by reason or emotion. By using the intellect, we are often able to identify the level from which an action came. There are times, however, when it may be impossible to determine from which level the action came because both may be operating simultaneously or else, we are unable to determine the total circumstances. However, much of the time we act without any conscious awareness of the level from which our actions come.

On the rational level, we perform a certain action because it makes good sense to do certain things a certain way. Our reason leads us to act according to rules and desired results. An illustration might help us. I was walking along when I noticed an unusual feeling in my foot. After a brief moment, I reasoned something was in my shoe that should not be there. I further reasoned that it made good sense to remove my shoe and extract the object that caused the pain. Upon removing the shoe, I found a tack sticking through the heel and insole. Since I was in my office, I had no way to remove the tack. Reason once again went to work. I could solve my immediate problem by separating the tack from my foot. I repeatedly folded a large piece of scrap paper, placed it in the bottom of my shoe over the tack and put my foot back into the shoe. The desired result was accomplished. A more permanent fix could come later. That is the nature of reason. It enables us to contemplate and carry out desired behavior for intended results.

The same illustration I used for the rational approach may also be used to illustrate the emotional approach. I was walking along and became aware of an "unusual feeling" in my foot. My response to that feeling could encompass not only awareness of pain but also much more. I could have responded emotionally to its presence or my inability to immediately fix it. I could have kicked and cursed over either or both. That would not eliminate the tack or the pain in my foot when I wore my shoe.

Emotional responses come in many sizes and from diverse causes. Suppose you are in a heated conversation and someone calls you a name that questions the marital status of your parents. Their comment does not cause physical pain, like the tack in the shoe, but it will cause emotional pain for most people. An emotional response is illustrated if you promptly "play telephone," i.e., you "reach out and touch someone" with your fist. Your action was motivated by emotion and not by reason, especially if the other person was much larger than you.

Something inside us may compel a response without our thinking about it. On the other hand, reason reminds us it is unwise to hit someone much taller and stronger than we. Also, regardless of the size of the other person or how hard we hit them, such a response seldom changes their opinion of our parents. We all have a personal example of a very emotional response. A young lover who left his date at the door after their first hearty goodnight kiss prominently displayed emotions by whistling and singing all the way home without thinking about his actions.

I worked with thousands of clients who had a severe pain in their gut. After personal research, extensive conversations and careful observations, I concluded the primary motivation for any abuse comes from the emotional level. An abuser's sickness and pain are initially in the emotions, not the intellect. The previously described model offers some added insight to what has happened to the abuser who no longer appropriately uses reason. Unhealthy results also come to those who are overly rational.

Emotions, or feelings, often become the motivating factor for much of life, even though the actions they ignite do not always make good sense. Any rehabilitation program or renewal process that begins with a primary focus on reason and intellect is doomed to failure. Most people firmly believe abuse makes no sense, especially when it destroys health, home life, holdings, honor, etc. Such destructive behavior seldom seems rational to anyone.

On the other hand, if abuse and inappropriate behavior are motivated primarily by feelings in the gut, by an attempt to find some relief, irrational behavior makes some strange sense after all. Abuse continues because it is a known source that provides some temporary relief for excruciating pain. A person feels compelled to act unwisely in order to resolve emotional pain, or find some temporary relief from it. Such behavior appears irrational to non-abusers but the abuser is driven to it. Long ago, I learned that most human behavior makes sense from some perspective, even if not to me at that moment. This interpretation of abuse is the only approach that makes sense to me and I believe it makes sense to the abuser. This interpretation destroys ingrained ideas and theories about abuse and the abuser and opens new doors to effective treatment and recovery.

Abuse, or any harmful behavior, normally originates as a response to unpleasant or painful feelings. A formula helps describe it. Abuse is an attempt to either get rid of an unwanted feeling or to get a desired feeling. Essentially, we have two sides of the same coin. In order to get something, we may have to get rid of something else, and vice versa. A person abuses something in an effort to extinguish the fire in the gut, to get rid of pain, and at the same time hopes to get a pleasant feeling they lack. Relief may be very temporary, but any relief is better than no relief. That is why people tolerate a painful aftermath. Relief that exacts a heavy price elsewhere is worth it.

All logical reasons against harmful behavior fade for the abuser because some welcomed relief is mandated, even if only for a little while. When a person in pain has found something that gives relief, even if temporary and costly, they are apt to try it again when they want additional relief. Repeated self-medication for continuing pain may lead to abuse and abuse may lead to addiction. The initial pain may be physical or emotional. Advanced abuse of drugs and alcohol illustrates unwise behavior and is further complicated by the addictive properties of both. Addiction increases the unwise behavior and may ultimately increase the pain but one has become subservient to the new "god," as our model depicts. I suspect the process is very similar for any abusive or harmful behavior.

Abuse and harmful behavior are conceived and birthed in the emotions. If that is not the point of conception, it is the seedbed in which they take root and the soil in which they grow. Several things guided me to that conclusion. I conducted a particular exercise with hundreds of patients in treatment centers. During small group meetings, I asked participants to state why they or someone they knew abused drugs and alcohol. I recorded every stated reason on a chalkboard as they gave them. I offered no help and gave no answers of my own. When they ran out of answers, I asked the participants to tell me which of their reasons were rational and which were emotional. Almost without fail and with no encouragement from me, the patients decided every reason they gave was an emotional expression.

On a rare occasion, someone argued that their reason was rational, only to have the group point out the error in their judgment. The groups, composed of abusers and addicts, knew what motivated their behavior. As a non-abuser of drugs and alcohol, what could I say to contradict their conclusions? It was the only thing that made sense.

Personal research and observation proved to me what I had long suspected. People abuse drugs and alcohol because of feelings. If that is true, it is only one step further to suspect that all abuse comes from the same motivation. Should other harmful behavior be any different? All are birthed at the feeling level and all are practiced to get or to get rid of certain feelings Even though abuses may differ in name, the feelings that birthed them are amazingly similar. Sexual abuse, child abuse, over eating, workaholics, etc., fit the pattern. Religious fanatics are also included because irrational exuberance in religious talk and action is ultimately geared to get or to get rid of certain feelings.

The common seedbed for all abuse and addiction reflects the close kinship of all humanity. People in our society have repeatedly suggested abusers of drugs and alcohol are very different from the rest of society and have looked down on them with great disdain. People who are commonly called "abusers" are fundamentally no different from the rest of us because we are all made from the same fabric and put together from the same pattern.

Some of us learned how to appropriately deal with the pain in our gut and some of us did not. That is our primary difference. Abusers of drugs and alcohol are brothers and sisters of all humanity, including all other abusers, and we are they. Since most of us abuse something, or have a strong tendency to do so, none of us have bragging rights to being perfect. All of us, identified and unidentified abusers, are less than perfect. We all could mend our model.

Feelings are a vital and necessary part of our life. Without them we would cease to exist as human beings. We cannot over emphasize that fact because few people really believe it. For too long, folks have consciously and subconsciously taught their children, especially the males, that feelings are not important and should be ignored much of the time. It is time to dethrone that theory and stress the importance of feelings because they are the primary motivation for human behavior. I read about a psychiatrist who knew the crucial importance of feelings and how they affect us from infancy to old age. He asked each patient to tell him their earliest memory and their present attitude about life. One man recalled sitting on the floor, as a young child, in a dirty diaper and his mother waving a wooden spoon over his head while threatening to beat him with the spoon if ever he dirtied his diaper again. A woman remembered playing alone on the floor. Her mother rushed into the room, took the child in her arms and ran out the door. As they hurried outside, the mother explained there was a gorgeous sunset she wanted the child to see. The man's adult attitude about life, he said, is like sitting in a dirty diaper waiting for someone to hit him with a wooden spoon. The woman's present attitude sees life as an exciting adventure, looking for and anticipating the next beautiful sunset.

These two illustrations emphasize the direct correlation between powerful childhood feelings and one's general attitude about life. Feelings cannot be continuously denied or ignored. Any extended attempt to do so is perilous to the person who attempts it.

Many personal problems arise and are encouraged because we are conditioned to ask improper questions. This is especially true when we talk about feelings. The primary question, we were told, is, "How can I prevent having feelings about certain things?" The question encourages a denial of our feelings and further suggests something is wrong with us if we have them.

Having been saturated with that idea, we may feel bad even when we are feeling good! Most of us will have feelings that cannot be prevented or truthfully denied. If we were taught to have no feelings about certain things or to hide them if we do, it is quite natural to assume something is wrong with us when we have them, thereby causing additional feelings and providing the seedbed for future problems.

That improper admonition has created extensive and unnecessary misery. We must find another response to our feelings or suffer the consequences. There is a more appropriate question that facilitates health, wholeness and healing. It is, "How can I recognize and appropriately respond to all my feelings which naturally come to me as a person?"

The second question offers a much more positive and helpful approach by affirming at least two truths. First, it proclaims the unavoidable existence of multiple feelings. Second, it confirms the appropriateness for a person to have them. It further affirms a person may be unaware of present feelings and it may be necessary to uncover them and wrestle with them before health and wholeness are restored. If these two truths were permanently instilled into the mind of all children and adults, abuse would be radically reduced. Parents and other resource persons constantly model which basic question about feelings they deem most important, thereby enticing others to follow their lead.

The conviction that it is natural and normal to have numerous feelings, and that it is helpful to admit having them, goes against what many of us were taught from childhood. Many people consciously and subconsciously taught us by word and by model. My two grandchildren provided a perfect illustration of how young children respond to what they see and hear. Our daughter called them from play to accompany her on a trip in the car. Our grandson, age seven, was upset because his play was interrupted. He sat in the back seat and cried. Our granddaughter, age five, sat in the front seat. She leaned over the seat, pointed her finger at her brother and said, "Big boys don't cry." Many previously discussed issues are encompassed in that event. It is helpful to notice the age and sex of the child who made the statement, to whom it was made and from where it originally came. No doubt, it was used here and elsewhere as an attempt to be helpful.

For years, male children in particular have heard that exact statement. Most of us have heard or used it. We can easily see the difficulty created by that well-intended statement. Picture a young bare-foot boy who has just torn off a toenail when he stubbed it on a big rock. The most natural thing in the world is to cry when hurt.

However, some well-meaning adult offered comfort by saying to him, "Big boys don't cry." He was in a painful predicament. He hurt and wanted or maybe even needed to cry but he also desperately wanted to be seen as a big boy in the eyes of others and himself. He was in a "no win" situation, regardless of which choice he made. "Being a big boy" will eventually carry the most weight.

Early in life, it becomes more important to be a "big boy," even when he is seriously injured, loses someone he deeply loves, becomes guilty of some grave error, etc. Repeatedly he is told, and he finally believes, if he is a big boy he must not cry, regardless of the circumstances or the source of his pain. The prohibition against crying goes with him throughout life, even though crying is a normal human response to severe pain.

This is tragic and the outcome could have been easily altered had some understanding person said to the young boy in pain, "I am so sorry you hurt. I will comfort you during your pain and I will help you deal with it." For several reasons, this type response is revolutionary, compared to "Big boys don't cry." First, it acknowledges where the sufferer is, i.e., in pain. Acknowledgement immediately makes one feel better. Second, it admits the appropriateness of being there and the person in pain is not castigated for admitting they are there. Third, it is positive, not negative. Fourth, it creates no additional or lingering pain to be confronted in some fashion at a later time. Fifth, it offers meaningful assistance to someone in need, validating their worth and their world. If those offering assistance to others in pain followed this positive approach, abuse would be greatly curtailed, especially since the negative approach is abusive itself.

There is a frightening story illustrating the difficulty some people have when big boys are caught crying. If it is not authentic, it is a superb illustration. A middle-aged man married a woman who had a teenage daughter living with her. Shortly after their marriage, the new stepdaughter began to date a young man who was well known by the stepfather.

The relationship between the two young people became more intense. The stepfather knew the young man had serious problems and was not an ideal date or mate. Desiring to prevent pain for the new stepdaughter, he calmly informed her what he knew about her close friend.

She hastily and forcefully replied, "For eighteen years I have managed quite well without you telling me who my friends should be and I want you to know I can go eighteen more years with no help from you."

The stepfather, deeply concerned over the delicate matter, decided to discuss it with the girl's mother, his new bride. He calmly told his wife what he knew about the daughter's close friend and his own concern for her future health and happiness. It seems the daughter had learned well from her mother because the mother responded with almost identical words of the daughter. The husband tried again to convince the mother of the impending danger but to no avail. Defeated and totally dejected, he sat on the front steps of their home and sobbed uncontrollably for quite some time. After an hour or so, cops and men in an ambulance came, put him in a restraining white jacket with long sleeves and took him to the mental ward of the hospital where I worked.

This poignant story reflects a widespread belief that big boys don't cry, and if they do they get into serious trouble. A more profound truth is exactly the opposite. If big boys don't have the freedom to cry when they are in pain, they are likely to be in even bigger trouble.

In order to think more clearly about them, feelings can be divided into different types. There are probably professional labels for any type feeling we have but I chose my own. Four types surfacedmost often for people with whom I worked. The first is "repressed" feelings. The dictionary tells us "repress" means to prevent the natural and normal expression or development of something, to suppress by force. I believe many feelings are consciously and subconsciously pushed beyond immediate awareness. That may not be totally inappropriate.

For many reasons, we harbor feelings without being immediately aware of their presence. In technical terms, repressed feelings may specifically refer only to those of which we are totally unaware. In layman's terms, repressed feelings also include those of which we are well aware and purposefully push back, deny, or avoid. There are times when we do not want or need to be reminded of a certain subject because it upsets us. Due to the pain it causes, we may seek to avoid subjects like a former spouse, a bad business decision, sexual indiscretion, death, abusive behavior, etc. However, anyone desiring health, wholeness and recovery must find ways to appropriately surface and deal with those feelings. Feelings buried beyond our ability to recall pose possible dangers and may need to surface before complete recovery comes. Due to what we were taught and due to much modern day thinking, that process is doubly difficult.

A fictitious male high school senior illustrates how we are prone to repress feelings. He had a couple of casual dates with a popular female classmate and liked what he saw. He decided to ask her to accompany him to the prom. He shared his plan with his best friend. The girl of his dream and he usually met at the lockers between the fourth and fifth period classes. Following the fourth period class, he rushed to the lockers with eager anticipation. He turned the corner and suddenly stopped in his tracks. The sight ahead of him made him sick inside. The handsome, tall quarterback of the football team stood leaning against a locker with an outstretched arm resting on top.

The girl he planned to ask to the prom stood underneath that outstretched arm, cuddled up close to the quarterback, making "goo- goo eyes" at him and grinning from ear to ear. The student who planned to invite the girl to the prom suddenly changed plans.

As he entered the fifth period class, his best friend yelled across the room, "Did you ask her?"

The hurting and heartbroken young man replied, "No. I decided not to ask her. She's not the girl for me. Besides, there may be someone else I'd rather ask."

Due to prior indoctrination, the deeply disappointed young man chose to repress his feelings and accept the consequences rather than tell the truth to a close friend. What does the future hold for this youth and others like him? How different his future would be if only he could tell the truth, admit his feelings, and receive validation from a friend. Within him, and millions like him, lies the seedbed of abuse. Is it too far-fetched to believe that much pain and abuse could be prevented if people could safely share their feelings without fear of reprisal?

I labeled the second type of feelings "unidentified." They are especially important when working with abusers. During the early stage of recovery, most clients will not immediately identify their feelings. A few of them may not know what they are. Some have never had an opportunity to consider the issue. Others are afraid to tell if they do know. At one time or another, all of us were unable to identify why we felt the way we did.

There were times when we knew we had a "squiggle in our gizzard" or a churning in our guts but we had no label for it. There may have been more times when our actions conveyed to others something was amiss and we did not know it or admit it. Recognition of the squiggles in the gizzard is crucial because they tell us something we need to know about our situation and ourselves. They are not accidental or independent. Even though unidentified, all of these feelings are important and some of them may be a fused bomb waiting to explode. We must admit their presence or identification is impossible. Recognition or suspicion of their presence may necessitate a serious "search and identify" mission, either alone or with competent help. Recognition, identification and appropriate disposition of the squiggles in the gizzard seriously affect recovery and continued health.

I labeled the third type of expressed feelings phony. The label describes what the feelings are, i.e., false, unreal, or inappropriate. Some people attempt to deny the reality of what they feel and pretend to feel otherwise. An elderly lady periodically visited my childhood home and we visited her. Most of us believed her husband was partially incapacitated from drinking too much moonshine whiskey. Apparently they were destitute.

During her visits, she constantly laughed, even when nothing was humorous. Tears ran down her cheeks when she laughed. She had nothing to laugh about and she was not happy. Her laughter appeared to be a cover. It was phony. To one degree or another, most of us have followed her lead. The hilarious times reportedly enjoyed by many of us, especially when we abused something or someone, may not be as funny as reported but perhaps we laughed to keep from crying. Perhaps we cry on the inside but dare not let it be known, especially if we believe "Big boys don't cry."

Displaying a phony feeling instead of a true feeling is not always accidental. Some of us were taught to act that way or else learned it was less painful to do so. Families frequently encourage and give permission for members to call one feeling by another name, thereby indicating it is legitimate to have one feeling but not another. A simple illustration shows how it works. A father put his young son in bed at his regular bedtime. Prior to drifting off to sleep, the lad heard the doorbell ring several times, loud voices and laughter. He reasoned, "They are having a party. I also like parties and I am very lonely upstairs when all those people are downstairs," He decided to join the party just as he entered the room his dad saw him, grabbed him by the arm, swatted his bottom and said, "Go back to bed."

Through tears, the lad protested and said, "Dad, I'm lonely." The father firmly replied, "You cannot be lonely in this house. Go to bed!"

A few weeks later the lad was in bed and again heard doorbells, voices and laughter. He was very lonely and upset over missing another party, but his dad let him know he was not welcome at the last one. His loneliness grew until he could tolerate it no longer.

He slipped down stairs and into the party. Just as he entered the room, his dad saw him, came toward him with fire in his eyes and said, "Boy, get back in that bed before I tan your bottom."

The lad stood still, began to cry and said, "Daddy, my stomach hurts."

The father doubted the lad's stomach hurt and knew the boy enjoyed parties, but what if he was slightly ill?

A wise bystander remembered what it was to be a lonely little boy, stepped forward, puts his hand on the lad's head and said, "I am so sorry you have a stomach ache. If your father doesn't object, perhaps some coke and cookies will make it better."

The lad's father reluctantly gave approval for him to have a snack. The lad liked that kind of medicine! After a good dose of it, he felt much better and willingly went back to bed. At first glance, it appears a bright lad outsmarted his dad. We actually saw a lad receive permission to call one feeling by another name.

In that family, one does not admit being lonely but it is quite legitimate to call loneliness by another name. The lad learns a lesson dad did not intend to teach. Many of us teach and learn similar lessons and those who learn such lessons ultimately pay a price Phony names may get you into the party but the hidden cost of using them can be enormous.

"Recognized" or "identified" is the fourth type of feelings I will discuss. An attempt to itemize all these feelings would be futile, lengthy and unnecessary. From that possible list, I will identify some that cause serious trouble for everyone and are most often problematic for abusers. One of these feelings is guilt.

Many of us say we have guilt but cannot precisely identify its nature. I have created a usable and helpful definition. "Guilt is having the present shackled by some past event, to the extent the present is robbed of its potential." It is a mental and emotional weight that keeps us from doing our best with what we have. Guilt is a heavy and painful burden carried by most of us at one time another. It is not a feeling peculiar to abusers but it is one most often discussed by them. We must overcome it before recovery is complete.

Abusers have an abundance of worry, which will not surprise anyone who knows anything about abuse. I also devised a working definition for worry that helps me better understand it. "Worry is having the present shackled by some possible and anticipated future event, to the extent the present is robbed of its potential."

Worry, like guilt, sucks possibilities from the present. Both are disabling. Serious abusers have numerous pending possibilities that are frightening and need immediate attention. Worry will not resolve a problem for them or anyone.

It ultimately creates more problems by diminishing existing abilities. The abuser is caught between two pressure points, possible problems arising out of past behavior or choices and the destructive response of worrying about them. Therefore, without competent help, it is so easy to resort to that which previously provided temporary relief. Recovery for one who worries extensively is like walking through a minefield. Possible danger awaits no matter which way they go. Extensive guidance may be necessary before a person learns how to properly deal with worry.

Low self-esteem is a common link connecting all abusers. I cannot recall confronting one abuser in a treatment program or in private counseling who did not suffer from it. Once a counselor has gained the patients' trust, most patients freely relate by word and action how they feel about themselves. Surprisingly, the majority of them express their feelings with four simple words, "I'm no damn good."

They mean precisely what they say. That opinion of themselves permeates the totality of their being. It possesses them to the degree that if they are on the verge of doing or being something that might question or deny that opinion, they will do something to prove to themselves and others that they really are no good. As long as an abuser holds that personal opinion, there will be no lasting recovery. That feeling devours all other positive things that might entice them to change.

They will not, possibly cannot, make a serious attempt to recover until they think more highly of themselves. Helping a person gain self-esteem is a long and complicated process, without simple and sure steps. To further complicate the matter, what helps one may not help another.

Numerous abusers expressed a strong sense of desperation, especially during advanced stages of abuse. They probably were plagued with it longer than they admitted. Many reported how desperate they were to find relief from a painful existence. They believed they could no longer tolerate the condition or situation. Suicide often enticed those who were extremely desperate, if only they were able to accomplish it.

They were willing to try anything, and they meant anything, in order to relieve the pain in their gut, which reflected a rational explanation for what others normally call irrational behavior. Moral teachings, religious doctrines, family practices, and civil laws provide little or no deterrent to anything that might diminish their pain. Even though they knew their choice was fraught with danger, they made it anyway. Their willingness to accept any consequences for their choice indicated the degree of desperation they felt. The recovery process must open new windows of hope and point to new and acceptable ways to resolve old feelings. Without personal hope, recovery is impossible.

Every person has felt loneliness, fear, anger, hate, love etc. Heavy abusers apparently have great difficulty responding appropriately to these and other feelings. Apparently, if we are seriously out of balance in one area of our feelings, we are more prone to be unbalanced inother areas.

Our vast array of feelings may not be as compartmentalized as we thought. It appears they are connected in some way. A recognized or suspected problem with a particular feeling may be the tip of the iceberg signaling additional danger. If my theory is correct, this is another contributing factor that helps understand why some people became heavy abusers. Here is another indication of where the abuser is and where any meaningful recovery must begin.

I firmly believe a major portion of human behavior is motivated by feelings. At times, we are aware of those feelings at times we are not. My personal experiences with and observations of various abusers and addicts helped finalize that conclusion. Observation and study of wholesome and happy people indicated the same. I found it to be true in my own life.

Emotionally healthy people maintain a modicum of control over their feelings and may be able to rein them with reason. Emotionally healthy people recognize the importance of emotions and reason. Neither can constantly dominate without creating problems. Once feeling or reason primarily controls behavior, if either becomes our "god," serious problems are inevitable. Experience taught me that an abuser's life was derailed at the point when the pain in their gut dictated unhealthy behavior.

Recovery begins only at the point of pain. It also seems valid to conclude that much pain and suffering could be easily avoided if a child learns how to appropriately respond to feelings. How will they learn without a teacher? How will the next generation learn unless responsible people model by word and example? How and where will they learn until they hear and are shown that numerous feelings are a natural part of every person's existence, that it is helpful to admit having those feelings and that every one of them deserves an appropriate, rational and personal response?

It is quite common for us to have a pain in our gut that has nothing to do with a digestive disorder. It is somewhat comforting to know that each may have a genuine cause and a possible cure. With proper care, we may prevent their occurrence and we may guard against their reoccurrence. When present, they deserve our careful attention or else they may easily become the seedbeds of abuse.

CHAPTER 5

Who am I?

All of us live by certain rules, principles and a personal model. They reflect who we are. I know of no exceptions unless it is those suffering extreme mental illness. Many of us are not able to identify those underlying guidelines for life, but they are there.

One probable reason why we repeatedly experience disappointment, pain, stagnation, and failure is the inappropriateness of our model. We may not know who we are. Perhaps we need to change our opinion of who we are and how we should behave, especially if we are uncomfortable and unhealthy. Since our personal opinion of ourselves was first formulated in early childhood, when we knew little or nothing about what we were doing, it definitely deserves close examination if not change.

Most of us formulated our ideas from incomplete and incorrect information gathered from inaccurate and improper data provided by imperfect people. Those original answers created long ago tend to survive numerous forces that recommend change. Old answers have a way of holding on, even after we confront contradictory data. We frequently live by old information, even when new facts indicate change.

An ill and elderly gentleman demonstrated the compelling force of an old answer. His family took him to the psychiatrist because he insisted he was dead. The doctor tried several ways to convince the patient he was not dead, but could not. The doctor took a different approach.

He instructed the patient to go home and, twice each day for thirty days, look at himself in the mirror and say, "Dead men don't bleed."

Upon the patient's return to the doctor one month later, the doctor asked the patient if he had followed the order. The patient assured the doctor he regularly did what the doctor ordered, and more often than instructed. The doctor took the patient's finger, squeezed the end of it, stuck it with a needle and extracted some blood. The doctor lifted the patient's bloody finger and asked, "What do you say about that?"

The patient stared at the blood and replied, "What do you know, Doc? Dead men do bleed!"

We can be as persistent in our beliefs. All of us subconsciously formulated an opinion of ourselves very early in life. Since we are repeatedly confronted with additional data, it behooves us to consciously reconsider our early answers, especially if we presently lack health, happiness and wholeness. Revision is recommended when we experience serious pain in our gut and desire growth, maturity, and emotional health. All of us must make a revision in order to find health and wholeness, not just abusers and addicts.

There are numerous ways to discover what we presently think of ourselves. No particular way is necessarily better than another, as long as the job is accomplished without creating more harm than good. One point at which to begin is by seriously asking and honestly answering the question "Who am I?" Long ago, many of us allowed others to declare who we are without questioning their conclusion. If we want renewal and growth, it is absolutely necessary to answer for ourselves. Others may help us find an answer but it must eventually be ours or it has little lasting value for us.

Personal behavior strongly indicates our answer to this question. Behavior reflects our concept of who we are. Possible problems may arise at this point, especially if we behave differently than we profess. We may not recognize the difference in behavior and profession. A certain man reflected his lack of recognition when asked, "Why do you always answer a question with another question?"

He replied, "Do I always do that?"

Incongruent profession and behavior are often more prevalent in each of us than we are aware. One step toward uncovering our fundamental beliefs is to carefully compare our perceptions, our pronouncements, and our performance. We have some idea, perception, of what we believe about numerous subjects. When someone asks us what we believe about that subject, for various reasons, we may or may not tell them all we think or believe about it. However, over a period of time we, without fail, show what we truly believe and think, barring mental illness.

A fictitious illustration may help. Suppose my wife bought a new dress, brought it home and asked me what I thought of it. All married men know the danger in answering that question! In my mind I probably knew what I thought about that new dress. I also knew she bought it because she liked it and had a good reason to do so. I also knew she would wear it, not I. Truthfully, I did not care for the dress at all. Wanting to validate her, I replied, "It's fine," and nothing else was said.

Several days later we went out to dinner and she wore her new dress. During the evening I was unusually cross with her and finally spoiled the evening for both of us. Several days later, in another city, we were invited out to dinner and she had the audacity to wear that dress again. The evening eventually ended as before when she wore the dress. It is possible to say we have no idea why both evenings ended as they did and we could be correct. However, the reason both evenings ended as they did may have been caused by her wearing a dress that I thoroughly disliked but had told her, "It's fine."

I had difficulty acting as if I liked the dress when deep inside, I hated it. Therefore, I punished her and myself with my behavior that reflected what I really believed about her dress, regardless of what I said. To further complicate the issue, my response could have been at the subconscious level! It is possible I said, "It's fine," and thought it was! Actions revealed my true belief.

If I want to know what I believe or think, I should seriously observe my behavior. One isolated incident, illustrated with the new dress, proves very little. Repeated incidents of a similar nature indicate trouble and the trouble may be with me. This is true for everyone, but abusers and addicts may find this extremely enlightening as well as a simple way to begin recovery. If my behavior stinks and is inconsistent with what I say I believe, I need to purposefully harmonize my beliefs and actions. If there is unnecessary pain in my life, perhaps I should look here. "Who am I?" I am someone who ultimately reflects what I believe by what I do.

There are other processes by which I may gain insight into "Who am I?" One is to write the epitaph I want on my tombstone. There is something rather sobering about this activity. If seriously done, it gets to the heart of our question. The finality of our own death and our legacy encourages openness and honesty. Thoughtful and honest epitaphs apparently capsulate the essence of who we believe we are and reflect possible action.

A remarkable epitaph came to my attention during a military gathering. I regularly facilitated a program designed to help recruits discover who they were. I often asked them to write their own epitaph as a part of that process. On a very hot Texas summer afternoon, I met with a group of about two hundred recruits in the corner of a chapel that seated a thousand. I instructed them to write their own epitaph. After they completed it, I gave participants an opportunity to share what they had written. After some strong encouragement from her associates, one young female recruit stood. A quick glance at her left no doubt that she was a female!

She said, "Here lies the bones of Cynthia Jones. Her life, it held no terrors." At that point she stood erect, extended her well-defined chest upward and outward, and loudly exclaimed, "Born a virgin." She then relaxed, leaned slightly forward, dropped her shoulders and slowly said, "Died a virgin. No hits, no runs, no errors."

We, like her associates, may laugh at what she said. A close examination of her words revealed volumes about how she saw herself and her guidelines for life. I recommend this exercise for fun and helpful insight. What you learn may surprise and enlighten you. Another way to uncover "Who am I?" is to honestly answer the question in as many areas as possible. A simple and factual answer can produce a wealth of helpful information for revising our opinion, especially if the opinion is seriously asked.

Giving serious consideration to something as simple as our name may reveal new possibilities. I am someone who was given a name by my parents. Names are considered less significant now than they once were. In ancient times, they often were symbolic and frequently carried a message. The Bible contains many examples.

Modern names seldom contain symbolism or messages as in ancient times. Our name may reflect parental dreams for us to imitate those after whom we were named. Our name may be one that is honorable and historic. It may be especially meaningful to parents for numerous reasons and they hung it on us because we were special to them.

Whatever our name, it is very special and was given to us because we were something special when we received it. I sometimes wonder if there is any connection between my name, Joseph, and the fact that I became a clergyman. I have no awareness of a connection but I do not deny the possibility.

Along with my given name I inherited a family name as a part of my birthright. Having told someone our family name, they usually want to know from which bunch we came, the ones across the river or town or state, etc. We cannot escape the consequences of being tied to those with a like name. We can seek to separate ourselves from the bunch with a bad reputation, identify with the good guys, and build a good reputation by our behavior.

There are added advantages in being from the honorable bunch, but if we aren't it need not defeat us. If we have the misfortune of being from the dishonorable clan, we can partially overcome its impact by wholesome living. The struggle to gain a better reputation may be difficult at first but it may be surprising how quickly the change will come when we work at it.

I fortunately inherited an impeccable reputation from my father. I fondly remember one particular occasion that proved his reputation and did wonders for mine. During my late teens, he wisely allowed me to have my own crops, livestock and money.

We needed some fertilizer for the farm. I went after it. I asked the storekeeper if he had a particular kind and he assured me he had more than I wanted. I then asked if he would accept a check from me.

He jerked his glasses down on the end of his nose, looked over them at me, a sixteen- or seventeen-years old lad, and said, "Boy, who in the world are you?"

I stood erect, extended my chest, and firmly replied, "I am Joseph Way, son of O.L. Way."

He hastily shoved his glassed back into their proper places and said, "Hell, give the boy anything he wants."

There is power in a name, some of which we inherit and some of which we bestow. A certain amount of baggage always comes with our birthright and we can make it better or worse.

Who am I? In this modern and sophisticated age, I not only have a name but I also have several numbers belonging exclusively to me. Each of my numbers is specifically reserved for me and distinguishes me from any other person with the same or similar name. Numbers may be considered impersonal but they are important. The presence or absence of certain numbers provides profound insight into who I am. I need my numbers because I am unique and deserve a special identity.

Who am I? I am a human being and that makes me very special. It separates me from the multitude of other things that exist in this gigantic universe. The meaning and ramification of being human allow various interpretations. However, most of us recognize we are unique creatures. Some of us may appear more unique! Even though there are billions of other human beings and billions of other things in the universe, there is nothing among them exactly like any one of us. I have certain characteristics common to other people and things but no single one of them is exactly like me. I must affirm my differences and my uniqueness to fully claim my identity. As a human being, I am unique and I am very special, regardless of my history, status or present behavior.

Our two most distinguishing human traits are intellect and emotion, the ability to reason and make emotional responses. I am aware of my existence and have some feelings about it. We are apparently the only creatures in the universe who blush, thus reflecting both thought and feelings. These two traits place a giant gulf between the remainder of the universe and us.

When that gulf is narrowed, it is usually because we move away from those traits and not because the rest of the universe moved closer to us. Someone jokingly said that it took a million years for a monkey to evolve into a human but it takes only a few minutes to reverse the process. There may be more truth here than we want to admit.

Abuse, especially of drugs and alcohol, has a devastating effect precisely at this point. Excessive abuse robs us of our unique ability to think clearly and to recognize what we feel. Persons under the heavy influence of drugs and alcohol have done things that no other creature in the universe would dare do, possibly renouncing and maybe severely injuring their own humanness. Intellect and feelings enable us to claim a special spot in the universe but we must choose how we use them.

I am one whose nature is to love and to be loved. Love is the nourishment that enables proper human growth and health. Improper love produces atrophy and death, perhaps gradually and painfully. Without love, we may breathe and exist for a long time but it is questionable if we are really alive. Love gives meaning to life, from the cradle to the grave. Those who do not receive love and who cannot give love exist with little meaning or real pleasure.

Life-giving love is hard to define or describe. In essence, it is wanting for someone, self and others, what is best for them to the extent we are willing to work and suffer in order to bring that to fruition. Every person is born with the innate ability to receive and to give that kind of love, when given a chance. Due to harsh circumstances and bitter experiences, a person may doubt they can ever be loved or give love. That natural human trait can be restored and exercised in almost any person. Proper love of self and others and being loved properly are prime motivating factors for productive human behavior. People who receive love tend to give love and to be creative in giving. Those who do not receive or give love tend to be destructive, to themselves and others. Proper love is the unique source for healthy and wholesome living. It is available to me and to everyone because we are human. I can love and be loved because of who I am.

Who am I? I am who circumstances and events allowed me to be. In many ways, diverse circumstances determined who I am. I had absolutely no control over many of them. No one offered me a choice of parents, the color of my skin, my sex, the time of my birth, the conditions in the world, etc. Each and all of these were very influential in my life and yours.

I am a child of formally uneducated, southern, rural parents who birthed me in the closing years of the depression, thereby placing me in a niche that nudged me toward becoming who I am. Members of minority groups have been denied certain privileges and positions open to others. They also could not control many of the circumstances associated with who they are.

All of us have a personal story of uncontrolled circumstances that affected us. Some effects were for good and some for less than good. It is helpful to identify those circumstances and to clarify their impact upon us. Identifying and clarifying those circumstances should proceed slowly, carefully, and without judgment. Even though some of those circumstances denied access to certain things we believed important, they may have provided us with other things of greater importance. As an example, my family had few worldly possessions but I was able to go to a local bank and get a large loan without collateral. My name was more valuable than possessions. The negative side of certain circumstances can be as strong as the positive side, if not stronger, and may hold the key to understanding who we are.

Who am I? I am what other people allow me to be. People, like circumstances, exerted uninvited, unrecognized and extensive control over our life, in our formative years and beyond. The attempt to control is sometimes subtle and meant to help.

A young chaplain under my supervision introduced his infant son to me as a "future preacher." That father sought to determine whom his son became. I wonder what will happen in a few years if that son has no inclination to be a preacher, other than knowing his dad desires it. I am also concerned over what will happen if at some point the boy thinks he has little or no other choice.

On another occasion, my wife and I visited a family and the husband was not home. Their son, a high school senior, and I sat in one room and the women in another. I asked about his plans for college and a career. He got excited and eagerly enumerated his desires for both. Suddenly, from the adjoining room came the forceful voice of his mother.

She said, "You know where your father and I have decided you will go and you know what we have decided will be your major." She then named the college and his major subject, neither of which agreed with what he had eagerly shared.

He looked at me and I looked at him and we changed the subject. The excitement left him when someone sought to control his life.

A young prospective bride and groom met with me to discuss a pending wedding ceremony. We shared possibilities, preferences and procedures. Once I had an understanding of what they desired, I began to outline the ceremony.

Suddenly the prospective bride said, "Oh no, we can't do that."

Shocked, I asked if I had misunderstood their wishes.

"No, it's not that," she said. "That's what we want but Mama told us how it will be done or else she won't pay for it."

We designed the ceremony according to the wishes of the bride's mother.

Unless things change, when this bride's daughter plans her wedding, it will be as this bride wanted and was not allowed to have. Where and when will it stop? We are frequently what others allow us to be.

Several of my college classmates appeared rather miserable much of the time. It seems they came to that college because it was the one their parents chose and the one for which their parents would pay. Many of those students had no idea what they wanted to do or be. There is no reason to wonder why many of them did poorly, failed, or just quit.

Apparently, they were not ready or willing to break the parental strangle hold under which they lived. Before we condemn them or any of the others mentioned above, let us closely examine ourselves for signs of parental control exerted over us during our youth and long after we left home. At first glance, it may appear almost insignificant. Upon closer examination, it may have controlled a big portion of our life. Each of us has our own example. In my childhood home, we were not allowed to shoot a gun on Sunday unless a crow got in the pecan tree or a hawk got after the chickens. Almost seventy years ago, I left that home to make my way in the world but I did not leave its influence. After high school, college, graduate school, numerous additional courses and two retirements, there is an instant squigglein my gizzard if I pick up a gun on Sunday! Make no mistake, we arewhat others allow us to be, until we decide to change.

Who am I? In matters that count most, I choose who I am and who I will be, within certain limits. It is not accidental that I address the matter of choice after the other answers were given. All the other answers to "Who am I?" come from outside and beyond me.

The final answer must and will always come from within. This fact does not negate the importance and impact of all the other answers. They provide a framework from which the final answer must come. Situations, circumstances, and other people periodically, if not permanently, control some options open to me and thereby limit the range of available choices.

However, they do not destroy the opportunity or necessity for me to make choices in light of where I am and who I want to be. I cannot refuse to choose. My only option is the type of choice. If I choose renewal, it is urgent for me to understand all I can about those other answers so that I may now wisely choose what to do in response to them.

Regardless of what those other answers are, it is my responsibility and opportunity to consciously shape them to the best of my ability. A wise person does not sit and say, "Woe is me," but rather deliberately chooses what to do with life, now that he or she better understands their history.

Since we didn't absolutely control much that shape us, we consider any perceived imperfection, in our history and us, a flaw, that may or may not be the truth. It is easy to blame others for our imperfections. We find some solace when we remember flaws are a natural part of our humanity. We all have them. That does not make them less problematic or painful.

Imperfect conditions and circumstances are more prominent for some of us than for others. Some of us conveniently use flaws as an excuse to justify present behavior.

It is also true that we are not fully responsible for many of them. Regardless of the source of imperfections in our history and us, we are responsible for overcoming as many as possible or they will not be overcome.

I did not choose everything that shaped my existence to this point in my life but that does not free me from choosing for the future. I must choose to live in the shadowy aftermath of my perceived and present imperfections or I must choose to move beyond them. They do not completely overshadow my past unless I allow them to do so. By far, they are not the only source from which I can build my future.

For the majority of us, there were and there are many beneficial and positive circumstances, situations and people that we must not overlook or forget. In order to find them it may be necessary to change where and how we look at them and ourselves. Consciously viewed from a new perspective, the flaws may not appear as detrimental as we once thought. From this day forward, I am who I choose to be, within certain limits, regardless of what I was or from where I came. Who am I? Without any doubt, I am a composite, formulated from what I received and what I chose. It can be no other way. Unless I am careful and thoughtful, I will be more of the former than the latter. Regardless of how it may first appear or what I desire, in the

final analysis, it is always the latter because I make the choice. Blind and subconscious acceptance of the former almost guarantees our life will remain less than fulfilled. That is a choice. Joyful acceptance of the latter provides hope, strength and possible fulfillment.

Previously, I may have been unaware of what was thrust upon me from outside or its impact upon me. From this point forward, it behooves me to carefully contemplate what came to me, what I allowed it to do to me and what I choose to add or subtract from it. In order for me to better understand my present condition, it is essential for me to carefully examine my history. A keen awareness of my history and my present will assist me in consciously choosing my future. Who we presently are is one thing but whom we choose to become may be something very different. Most of us desire improvements. If we are not yet who we desire to be, our personal history or present condition need not overwhelm us. It is unwise to harshly judge who we are. We may have done exceptionally well with the opportunities we had. If there is a need or desire for change, everything we need is readily available.

The garbage in us can be dumped or recycled. Whatever we need but do not have can usually be acquired, either through our own efforts or with the help of others. Skin color, lack of formal education, abusive parents, abusive behavior, extensive successes, etc., are not reasons to remain as we are. Previous destructive conditions and present circumstances cannot completely imprison and defeat us unless we choose to capitulate. Powerful people cannot totally control us without our permission. Ultimately, the answer to "Who am I?" is always given its final shape, dimension and force by what I choose from available options. Within certain limits, I am who I choose to be.

CHAPTER 6

What Do I Think of Me?

I am amazed at the inordinate amount of time many of us spend carefully asking and then frantically answering inappropriate questions. I am also fascinated by how quickly major problems are frequently solved when appropriate questions are asked and answered. Having made this discovery, I determined long ago to help others first focus on finding the proper questions related to their stated problem. If I was as helpful as many have suggested, it was due to this approach.

Abuse and recovery are definitely connected to asking and answering questions. Abuse comes more frequently from inappropriately answering appropriate questions than from answering no questions. Recovery of every kind is related to honestly and consciously answering appropriate questions.

Answering crucial questions is not always a conscious process but they get firmly answered just the same. Some unconscious answers have the power to control our life. All of us subconsciously answered many questions, at least initially. After years of work as a counselor and therapist, I have concluded there is one crucial question that holds the key to any renewal process. It is one of those questions we initially answered at the subconscious level. It must be consciously answered if we want recovery and wholeness.

That critical question is, "What do I think of me?" The significance of this simple sounding question is enormous because its answer largely determines how we daily live. Positive thoughts about myself will likely produce positive feelings about myself that tend to produce positive behavior. Negative thoughts about myself will most often lead to negative feelings about myself that result in less than constructive behavior. The way I think affects how I feel. The way I feel affects how I live. Given these facts, it seems wise for each of us to review and consciously recognize the guide by which we daily live. At some point during my work in drug and alcohol rehabilitation, I had an inclination of a definite connection between abuse and what a person thought of himself or herself. In order to test my assumption, I collected specific information from every new patient during my initial interview.

I gathered information on three hundred consecutive patients who entered the program. One or two questions normally asked at that time were designed to uncover precisely what the patient thought of himself or herself. To my astonishment, I did not have to probe for the information. Most patients gave the information early in the interview and many of them gave it without being asked. Their eager answer to the question was perhaps indicative of what others had said, or tried to say, to me if I had listened. It soon became obvious, and tabulations confirmed it, that every person used almost identical words to describe what they thought of themselves.

Most often they simply said, "I am no damn good." They were not only able to clearly and quickly state how they felt about themselves but most of them could also easily identify the time and circumstances when they first reached that conclusion. That conclusion most often came in conjunction with some major mishap, such as being severely beaten or abused by a parent or forceful separation from a family member by death, divorce, or adoption.

Some reached the same conclusion after what appeared to be less dramatic events. However, their convictions were just as firmly implanted as those who seemingly had a more traumatic experience. Different type experiences produced similar responses, strongly suggesting the severity of an experience is correctlymeasured by one's response to it. The above-mentioned study of the three hundred persons did not uncover one who thought highly of themselves!

My research was insufficient to prove the point but it appears that once a person concluded they were "no good" deterioration of life accelerated. They became more involved in questionable and unproductive behavior such as running away from home, stealing, skipping school, drinking, etc. In light of what was previously stated about "feelings," this is precisely what is expected after they formulated that conclusion.

They found the conclusion, "I'm no good," so painful they sought ways to make it go away. When it wouldn't go away permanently, they sought ways to ease the pain temporarily. Age and experience taught countless abusers that drugs, alcohol and other abusive behavior do precisely that. They did not consider the addictive nature of their solution. Their primary concern was temporary relief of the pain in their gut. For reasons unexplained and unexplored, seldom did anyone consider eliminating the source of their pain, even if they could.

I have no research to prove it but, until proven otherwise, I firmly believe that most, if not all, abuse is directly connected to what one thinks of herself or himself. Reasons for abuse are perhaps far more complex than any one person can comprehend but years of searching for a plausible explanation kept taking me back to this point. Finally, I decided to believe what the abusers told me because it was the only thing that made sense to them or me. Abuse appears to result from the person's own answer to the critical question, "What do I think of me?" The response was often influenced by inappropriate data, by what others allowed or encouraged and by circumstances they confronted but over which they had little control.

If our answer to this question is the pivotal point in life, each of us is greatly affected by whatever answer we give, whether consciously or subconsciously given. Furthermore, we are often unaware of how or when we first answered it. The awareness of my answer is a major key for understanding myself, for mending my model and for maintaining a healthy lifestyle.

Since recovery for abusers and addicts depends on changing their answer, it is highly possible that healing, health and wholeness are enhanced for anyone who carefully, deliberately and correctly reconsiders their previous answers. "What do I think of me?" is not an easy question for anyone to honestly answer. We can more easily guess what another person thinks of herself or himself, based on our observation of their behavior. It is sad when we know more about another person than about ourselves. Perhaps here is part of our problems in life. If we had the ability to see ourselves as others see us, we might easily answer the question. We are seldom encouraged to consciously answer such a question. Therefore, we have little experience and are often poorly equipped for the task. If this is true, we have some added insight to erratic behavior for others and ourselves.

Perhaps an illustration will help clarify some of the issues raised. I counseled a young female airman who had gotten into difficulty over her disregard for a specific military regulation. I encouraged her to put such behavior behind her, use her obvious mental abilities and friendly personality to perform her military duties and to progress in her career.

Within a short time, she was back for counseling on a similar matter. Again, I strongly encouraged her to mend her ways, concentrate on performing her military duties, get promoted and stay out of trouble. Within a few weeks she was back in my office after getting into serious trouble again. At that point, I had an insight. Even though she seemed perfectly capable of being an ideal airman, she would not and possible could not be until she changed her opinion of herself. It became obvious to me that she saw herself as "no good."

By flaunting her disregard for military regulations, she sought to convince others she was no good. My positive and encouraging comments did not help her and may have encouraged her to forcefully prove she was correct and not I. It was quite obvious that radical change was necessary or she would be discharged from the military. Later, I learned she was the product of a broken home, had been sexually molested by her father, and was raised primarily by her grandmother. Her road to recovery, like so many others, ran through a new answer to an old and basic question, specifically, "What do I think of me?" We may now have a clue to erratic and irrational behavior demonstrated by abusers who were in apparent remission for many months or even years.

Without any warning or explainable reason and when everything was apparently going quite well for them, they suddenly returned to their old lifestyle. Those closest to them may wring their hands and ponder what could have been done to help. Relatives and associates ask, "Why did they do it?"

There is probably no single answer and hundreds of answers may not be enough. My simple answer is the person abused again to reaffirm they remained "no good." The reaffirmation was for others and for himself or herself. Had they continued without abuse and unacceptable behavior; they would have to change a basic belief about themselves. They had to many painful memories, too many erroneous assumptions, too much misinformation and too much present pain for them to conclude otherwise.

The conviction that they are "no good" had been buried so deeply within that they were compelled to forcefully declare it once more by action. The conviction and feeling that they are "no good" won again and it will always win as long as it is present. Healing and recovery will come only after they develop a model for life that affirms their personal worth.

Statistics indicate abusers must develop a new opinion of themselves before recovery is possible. I do not place complete confidence in statistics related to substance abuse and recovery. From where I have worked and from what I have seen, there is no way to keep accurate statistics because it is impossible to track all patients who leave a program. Furthermore, no one knows how many other abusers exist, their location or what happened to them. If statistics on abuse have any validity, they certainly frighten us.

During my days as a therapist, statistics indicated for every thirty-six alcoholics, one got and remained sober. The other thirty- five came to an untimely death. Another set of statistics indicated for thirty-six people who completed a drug rehab program, twelve will be drug free, twelve will be dead as a result of using and twelve will be using after five years. I have my doubts about the validity of those numbers but they alarming. I also believe a set of accurate statistics would be staggering.

If they tell us nothing else, these disturbing statistics indicate the difficulty of full recovery from substance abuse in particular and from abuse at any level. They also lend credence to what some have called

"The Death Wish Theory" for substance abusers. Having concluded that they are no good and feeling very lost and desperate, some serious abusers wish to die. They hurt badly, have no hope for life to improve, and expect matters to get worse. They therefore conclude they and the world would be better off if they were dead.

They may wish they were dead but since they firmly believe they are absolutely worthless they lack confidence in their ability to instantly kill themselves. If they are to get their wish, they must do it gradually or by putting themselves in dangerous situations that might accomplish that end.

I periodically confronted patients in treatment with this theory. Few of them argued against it. Many of those who did eventually changed their minds. Some declared our discussion helped them understand past irrational behavior. Some patients cited our discussion as a turning point in recovery and used it as a handle to pull themselves up. Given a chance to freely consider it, they decided a part of them did not really want to die, even if they had acted as if they did. That may partially explain why they had not totally destroyed themselves. I think some of them had a major change during our discussion and didn't recognize it. That may have been their first step toward recovery.

Many of those in and out of treatment have already experienced some type and degree of death, even though they continue to breathe. Many who are not physically dead are very sick and close to actual death. When life has lost its meaning and purpose, when dreams and desires no longer excite everyday behavior, when ambition and hope are gone, when one's innards ache from self-condemnation, is that not a form of death? Even as serious abusers painfully live, they also painfully die in many different and agonizing ways.

The fundamental question, "What do I think of me?" demands an answer. The truth may alarm us. It always gets answered by every person who is mentally and emotionally able to do so. The scary thing is that we often subconsciously answer it, allow someone else to give us the answer, or answer it from erroneous and incomplete data. Alcohol and drug abusers are by no means the only guilty persons at this point. All of us tend to be guilty for one reason or another. Regardless of who we are, an self-conscious and incomplete answer robs life of its potential and engenders suffering. Hope and help for all of us lie in an honest and deliberate answer.

Understanding our present answer to this fundamental question is not an easy task. The point at which to begin appears to be a careful analysis of our behavior. Since behavior is indicative of what we believe and who we are, it makes sense to direct our thoughts in that direction. Being human, we would probably profit most from using our unique traits of reason and emotion to examine our behavior. Other questions, asked and honestly answered, will assist us with our primary inquiry. My answers to them reflect my thoughts about myself.

The following suggested secondary questions serve as examples. Does my behavior support and compliment my chosen lifestyle and does it agree with my stated plan or purpose for life? Does my behavior agree with what I profess? Do I feel good about myself when I consider how I normally behave? What is my normal response to disappointment and stress? What is my normal approach to solving problems? On the basis of my behavior, what is the order of my first five priorities? How do others respond to my behavior? What kind of friends do I have and how long do I keep them? Why does anyone like or dislike me, after being around me for an extended period of time? What would the world be like if everyone acted as I act?

These and other similar questions will help us understand our behavior pattern that, in turn, will give a clue to how we truly see ourselves. Added insight may be gained by having someone we trust answer these questions about us and share their answers with us. Their perspective is not perfect but it may serve as a corrective for our own.

What I think of me may be partially revealed by ascertaining if I am primarily a positive or negative person. We all know both types. There are those who see a ray of sunshine in the darkest cloud and those who believe dark clouds are present on a perfectly clear day if you could see them. Those who expect things to go bad for themselves seem to see only the bad in others. If I am so negative in my thinking and expressed expectations that my imaginary friends refuse to visit, I do not think highly of myself.

An inebriated man came home on a cold and rainy night and illustrated a negative expectation. His clothing was soaking wet and he was chilled to the bone. His wife had already gone to bed but she left a glowing fire in the wood-burning fireplace.

When he got home, the fire was still going. He needed to get warm and dry so he lay down in front of the fire, possibly because he could not safely stand in front of it. Almost immediately he fell asleep. Soon thereafter, a burning log rolled from the fire and ignited his pants leg. When the heat aroused him, he raised his head to see what had happen. His state of mind and blurred vision did not help him correctly analyze the situation. After a brief look, his head fell back to the floor and he exclaimed, "Oh my! In hell, just as I expected."

Negative thinking and expectations color a person's outlook on life, blur their vision, and prevent them from seeing the positive things that happen or could happen if given a chance. Persons of this persuasion tend to practice personal put-downs. They repeatedly speak ill of themselves and emphasize past mistakes or failures. They seldom speak a positive word on their own behalf. A common comment from them is, "I never do anything right." These people may not get mad when others speak ill of them since they eventually expect others to see them as they see themselves. Persons who practice negative thinking may be encouraged to change, if shown they are not the only one who made mistakes.

Making mistakes is part of our humanity. We are not properly judged by the number of mistakes made but by what we do after making a mistake. Mistakes do not mean we are "no good" but rather that another approach will possibly be more productive. Mistakes may indicate diligent effort. They also provide unique opportunities for learning. Those who do nothing from fear of making a mistake are guilty of the greatest mistake possible.

Negative thinking and speaking lead to painful living. Positive, practical, realistic thinking and speaking hold hope for a brighter future for those who practice it. Positive, realistic thinking and speaking about ourselves enhance self-esteem and add zest to life. What we think of ourselves is reflected in what we repeatedly say and in how we say it.

Added insight into our opinion of ourselves comes from observing the way we respond to our history. Those who think poorly of themselves appear to be hung up on history, indicated by looking back and by living in the past. Those with high self-esteem seem to focus more on the present and future. Those who live in the past act as if they are stuck in reverse. We, like automobiles, need a reverse but to operate almost exclusively in that mode is not only living dangerously but also missing golden opportunities for growth and progress. New possibilities always lie in front of us, in the future, not behind us and in the past. For our lives and automobiles, it is very beneficial to use reverse at appropriate times but being stuck there is a real problem.

Fear of change and fear of the unknown convince some people that concentrating on the past is far less painful. Those hung up on history often live with constant worry and guilt, especially when their history was quite painful. Any added tragedy may be seen as further proof that they are truly "no good" and is only what they expected. If we are impaled by our history instead of anticipating and planning our future, we probably don't think highly of ourselves.

What I think of me is reflected in what or who controls my life. Is it another, some object or feeling, or is it I? How many of us can point to a dozen different things and truthfully say, "I did that because I really wanted to do it and freely chose it?"

Situations and circumstances tend to hobble and control us unless we learn how to break the shackles. Under the disguise of helping, well-meaning parents protect a child to the point it cannot protect itself and cannot function without their aid. Even after the child reached the age it should be able to do many things for itself, it cannot because it was and is controlled by others.

A man of my close acquaintance was undoubtedly the product of such a home. As an adult over twenty-five years of age, he had serious difficulty making a decision to act. If another person suggested he perform a certain task, he performed it well. Once that task was finished, he often stumbled about in circles until someone helped him identify the next appropriate task to undertake. His problem was not lack of intelligence but lack of experience and self-confidence.

From his youth, his father had given him no opportunity to think for himself, telling him every move to make, possibly including when to go to the bathroom and how long to stay. He lived at home several years beyond high school and spent time in the Army.

When separated from an outside control point, he had serious difficulty continuing on his own. I repeatedly pondered the process through which he went to get into that position. I doubt it was designed. Sadly, he is not the only person in that condition with whom I worked.

Countless clients shared with me the fact that something or someone had major control over their lives. Abuse, addiction, passion, habits, deep desires, past mistakes, plus many more things and people, called the cadence by which they marched. I also pondered the process through which they went to get into that position. There is no indication it was by design. Regardless of how it happened or what gave them their marching orders, almost without fail, they were very unhappy about it and did not think highly of themselves.

This does not mean that wholeness is achieved by being the absolute master of one's fate and the captain of one's soul. There is a mandatory middle ground where I can choose to do some things that please others and some things that appropriately please me. Persons who exercise major control over their lives think more highly of themselves than those who feel they are primarily controlled. There is probably an early and direct connection between those who are controlled and many of those who do not think highly of themselves. Which comes first is beyond my understanding and would be worthy of further research.

What I think of me is reflected in how quickly I do what I know needs to be done. Do I do it as quickly as possible or do I procrastinate? Those who set and follow schedule demonstrate basic control over their lives and tend to be more positive, less frustrated and more productive. Those who repeatedly procrastinate may do so because they doubt their ability to make a proper decision or to properly perform the task. Fear of something or someone prevents them from acting. Procrastinators look for the exact moment to act but it seldom arrives. For some reason, they apparently do not know when and how to act appropriately or else they cannot act even if they know.

Their explanation for the delay is, "I'm waiting for the proper time." What they often mean is, "I am a no-good person and cannot do this as it ought to be done."

Procrastinators have a built-in excuse for shoddy performance and failure because they believe they had inadequate time, information or material to succeed. Those who know how and when to continue, or who are willing to try, usually accomplish great things even when strong constraints are present. Emotionally healthy people are not immune to procrastination but it is not their regular routine.

Specific comments are in order for anyone who discovers or suspects they do not think highly of themselves. If you find yourself in that condition, it does not mean you are hopeless. It may mean there is now more hope than before because you uncovered the root cause of many problems. Once you know the cause of your problems you are better able to correct them. A positive point at which to begin is the realization that you can change, regardless of what you have been or have done.

Diverse circumstances and inexplicable situations helped place you where you presently are but they need not keep you there. You may have had little choice in many of them but you now must choose what you will do in response to them. Regardless of whether you want to choose or not, you have no choice but to choose a response. Your choice is to either continue as you are or make changes.

If you want to change. you can. Change may not be easy but it is possible. You may desire or need professional help but that is no disgrace and help is available. If change is desired and requires, begin by being as positive as possible. It is not egotistical to say forcefully and truthfully, "I am going to make changes."

Saying that is likely a change in itself. Small changes have gigantic effects over time. Begin with what is easy to accomplish, gain confidence and experience, and move to bigger things when you are ready or capable. Live in the present and focus on what is going on around you. Take charge of your life, where possible, with assurance and pleasure.

Begin with small and manageable elements and move outward and upward. Try to imagine how wonderful it will be when the "new you" bursts into bloom. Experience in your innards the joy of a new birth and the excitement that comes with each new success. Begin today to make changes because tomorrow may be too late. Life is too short to spend it in fear and pain, especially when you have at your disposal all you need to radically change it. The first step toward change is to say, "I can and I will" and then act accordingly.

Asking and answering proper questions eliminate waste of time and energy while opening doors to increased healing and wholeness. There is one fundamental question answered by everyone. The answer each one of us gives becomes the primary foundation upon which we build our life. If this question is that important, it is time we seriously, consciously and carefully answer "What do I think of me?"

CHAPTER 7

Trashing the Trash

With the possible exception of young children, every living person collects some private garbage with which they must deal. Politicians, preachers, peasants, the young and old and the rich and poor collect it. I have some personal garbage in my life and so do you. Collecting garbage is a natural part of our human experience. Learning how to handle that garbage is crucial to human health and wholeness.

If we all collect garbage, what is it we collect? Private or personal garbage is hard to identify. Garbage for one person is not necessarily garbage for another. Garbage in one situation may not be garbage in another. Personal garbage may be present but hidden from view or camouflaged. We can define it only in broad terms and general principles.

Generally speaking, it encompasses anything that diminishes human health and wholeness. We would be better without it. Ponder the contents of household garbage and draw a parallel with similar types of material in your life. What we say about one can be figuratively, if not literally, said about the other.

Both include such things as worthless junk, spent and spoiled materials, stuff that serves no valuable purpose and occupies space needed for more constructive things, plus items that contaminate everything they touch and even tend to spoil the container in which they are held. Personal garbage encompasses unhealthy thoughts, feelings and behavior that disrupt life's progressive flow. Personal garbage diminishes clear thinking, propagates inner pain and makes us undesirable company.

Heavy abusers and addicts are definitely not the only collectors of human garbage, regardless of what some would have us think. They certainly collect their share but that is not their distinguishing feature. Heavy abusers do not always have the most garbage but they tend to collect an inordinate amount. A more important question is not who has more garbage but rather what effect does the garbage have on those who possess it or, in extreme cases, who are possessed by it?

There are at least two valid reasons why some abusers could have more garbage at some designated point in time. The first reason is their present and previous lifestyle dramatically facilitates collection of garbage. A life primarily controlled by something other than clear reason and healthy emotions is destined to collect an inordinate amount of garbage. Heavy abusers of any type are included in this group but they certainly are not the only ones.

The second reason abusers have excessive garbage is they have no constructive way to get rid of it. Perhaps this is a clue to why they became abusers! If they collect less than others but do not properly dispose it, over a period of time they appear to have more, especially if others periodically empty their container. Regardless of who collects it, it accumulates and poses serious problems when there is no systematic disposal.

Heavy abusers may involuntarily contribute to the notion they have more garbage because they believe they do. By words, deeds and feelings they reiterate the ingrained conviction of "I'm no good." They not only tend to collect additional garbage but also may see themselves as garbage. Even though this is especially true for alcohol and drug abusers, they do not hold an exclusive franchise on that view.

Accumulated household garbage poses severe problems. Its presence and its distinguishing characteristics make it hard to hide and often cause unsightly clutter. Certain kinds have a way of announcing their presence in the neighborhood. Its presence inhibits, or sometimes prohibits, productive and desired behavior. Its abundance and continued presence may eventually poison the entire neighborhood and cause major problems.

Similar to household garbage, personal garbage has a way of forcefully announcing its presence in our lives. For numerous reasons and excuses, some of us deny its presence and delay any attempt to empty our garbage can. I was pleasantly surprised to discover serious abusers do not automatically deny and delay. Most of them immediately pour out their garbage if it is safe to do so. Without encouragement or probing, they hastened to empty their garbage, often on me. Once they felt it safe to do so, they openly spoke of trash and trouble within. Following some lengthy sessions, I felt as if I needed a bath to cleanse myself. Their garbage reflected their pain and often encompassed a portion of their problem. Based on my counseling experiences, I believe there is an innate urge to empty our personal garbage can. We have an urge to purge. Knowing when, where and how to appropriately get rid of our garbage is the real problem. The urge to purge was vividly illustrated by one particular client.

A lady phoned the office seeking an appointment with a chaplain. She was assigned to me. I discovered she was the wife of a military man and was a very active member of a local church situated outside the military base. She almost instantly began to pour out her garbage. She was involved in a lengthy extramarital affair and could no longer endure it. I am no prude and, as a career military man, I have heard and seen some rather rough stuff but the woman told me intricate details that almost made me blush.

After she had poured out her sordid story, I sought some way to help her. Since she was very active in a local church and deeply appreciated her pastor, I expressed my confusion as to why she told me, a stranger, her story. Why had she not gone to her pastor? She began to cry. After regaining her composure, she replied, "I had to tell someone but I could not tell my pastor or anyone else I expect to see again."

She demonstrated the compelling urge to purge her garbage. She is not the only person to do so. Hundreds of persons have done as she did, emptied the garbage when they had a chance and when it became too heavy to carry.

Looking back to her and many others, I realize they told me more than their stories. They told me how desperately they needed an opportunity to empty their garbage without it being flung back in their face. Too frequently, society has not offered that opportunity. Many of us, especially males, have been taught to share little or nothing of what is inside and certainly not private garbage. They told us, "Keep it all inside."

When anyone adamantly keeps garbage inside, pressure builds and the lid eventually blows off. They suffer because the garbage either stifles them, overloads them, or poisons their system, if not all three. There is an urgent need for our society to provide readily available and risk-free opportunities that allow persons to empty their garbage can. Since everyone has garbage and since it is often detrimental to health and happiness, persons must be encouraged and enabled to properly purge their system of it.

How do we purge ourselves of our garbage? Given the nature of garbage and garbage collectors, no simple step by step process guarantees its elimination. As in other areas, certain things may benefit one person and not another. Likewise, we cannot be very specific because every person and situation is unique. It is therefore necessary to offer suggestions that encompass general principles, realizing they must be tailored to fit the specific person who uses them.

A practical way to get rid of garbage is to dump it. We must remember that it can be dumped in more than one way and in more than one place. This reminder is a warning for us to be very careful when we initiate the dumping process. Like household garbage, it can be unceremoniously flung out the window or systematically deposited in an appropriate receptacle. It may be secretly or overtly shoveled into another person's pail.

Confession is one helpful process for purging. Genuine confession is frequently a therapeutic experience because it allows a person to dump some of their heavy garbage. I am not a Catholic but I have been favorably impressed with that church's effort to facilitate confession. Looking from the outside, it seems they previously had a more productive system than they presently have. In the past, anonymity of the confessor was carefully protected. As I understand it, some of that protection has been reduced. I wonder if people willingly confess today as they did in the past and if it is as helpful to Catholics as it once was. Protestant churches have not addressed confession in the same way. It is stressed by some but for most it is more of an individual thing or done as a corporate body.

Confession can be dangerous, especially if we confess to the wrong person. It is extremely important for us to confess to an appropriate person, one whose primary desire is to help the confessor. There is a story about three pastors of separate churches located in a small town situated a great distance from a city. The Catholic priest met weekly with the Methodist and Baptist pastors.

During one meeting, the priest said, "Being Catholic, I am accustomed to making a confession but being located far from a fellow priest, I have little opportunity to do so. I feel a need to confess so I will confess to you. I love to look at beautiful women. There is no lust in my heart but I sometimes make a special effort to look and enjoy. My church frowns on that."

Following some conversation among them, the Methodist minister replied, "I also need to confess. I like beer and when I am far away from my congregation, I am likely to have one. My church not only frowns on that but it could get me in trouble, so I need to confess."

The Baptist pastor had listened to every word spoken by the other two. After a long pause he said, "I also feel a need to confess. I cannot keep a secret and I cannot wait to tell your parishioners what you have told me."

I confess that you can change the denominations to fit your preference! Confession can be dangerous but, when done appropriately, it has the potential to remove much of the garbage. Experience, common sense and simple questions will help locate someone to whom a confession can be safely made.

For various reasons and circumstances, some people laboriously drag their garbage with them for years and may even fight to protect it. Life would be much more productive and far less painful if only they could appropriately dump it. In order to do so, some of them will need professional help. Others only need an opportunity and encouragement. Old garbage is often tied to persons who are no longer alive, making it much more difficult to dump.

A lady in the course I taught at a Spiritual Life Conference was standing by a swimming pool, conversing with other participants. Someone acted as if they were going to throw her into the pool. She went berserk. After she regained some of her composure, I spoke with her. Years earlier, her two sons drowned on the same day. They went for a swim, as they often did, but one did not give her a chance to tell him she loved him because he was mad at her. Since that time, she could not go into deep water. For years she continued to carry the agony of not telling her son she loved him that one final time. She desperately needed to get rid of the garbage connected to that experience but he was no longer alive.

Her story illustrates the untold experiences of countless others who harbor unresolved agony over unfinished business with deceased persons. Some have successfully purged the garbage by writing letters to the deceased in which they say what they wish they had said long ago. Others found relief by speaking to a surrogate for the deceased. Improperly dumped garbage may disappear for a time but it is likely to return, accompanied by its kin. Some people dump their garbage on others who have no need for it or knowledge of what to do with it. The ungrateful receiver frequently flings it back, with extra added! A garbage-throwing contest can develop into a nasty thing. Communal and personal problems are pathetically prolonged when individuals or groups try to throw more garbage than they received.

Some people believe they should defend themselves by throwing garbage. I read about a strange beetle with a sack attached to its rear end. The beetle constantly carries juicy fecal matter in its attached container. Certain ants love to eat those beetles. When an ant approaches a beetle, the ant first feels of his intended feast to see if it is prime quality. As the ant examines his possible treat, the beetle flings the fecal matter into the ant's face. The beetle escapes when the ant pauses to clean himself.

Symbolically speaking, there are people who look for an opportunity to imitate the beetle but the recipient of their gift is not likely to imitate the ant. In such situations, heated arguments may arise over who first flung the dung! During such fights, and at other times, ingenious ways are devised to throw the garbage. No matter how fast or far we fling our garbage, we must properly dispose of it or else it creates more.

Persons who have no known place to properly dump their garbage may need encouragement to respectfully use another person's dumping place and process until they find one of their own Adequately trained counselors and emotionally healthy people know how to handle other people's garbage without reprisal. They also know how to gently suggest processes and places that may be beneficial to the uninformed. The world desperately needs people who can serve in this capacity. They would relieve a vast amount of suffering and eliminate the origin of much more.

Another way to get rid of garbage is to recycle it. Recycling is a modem day necessity for household garbage and is also a marvelous idea for ridding ourselves of personal garbage. My next-door neighbor removed a wooden bed frame from a bus he converted into a motor home for his large family.

He said to me, "I wish the garbage man would remove that thing from my lawn."

I replied, "Leo, I will be happy to play garbage man."

After taking it across the street, I sawed off one small piece of board, added a few additional ones and painted it. We set it under a picture window in the living room and used it as a large bookcase.

Several days later, Leo was sitting in our living room and commented on how he liked the new bookcase. "I really need one like that," he said. "Were did you get it?"

I first thought he was joking but realized he was not. After learning what it was, he commented, "I'm tempted to take it home with me because it was originally mine."

This story reiterates the fact that one man's trash is often another man's treasure. This may be true for household trash but normally not true for personal trash. However, personal trash may hold the seed of some treasure and may become a seedbed where other things will grow if the trash is properly recycled.

Abusers and addicts repeatedly amazed me with their uncanny ability to acquire drugs and drinks, even when they had no money or when others desperately sought to keep it from them. On more than one occasion, I complimented them on their ability to do that and I challenged them to recycle that effort and ingenuity toward remaining clean and sober. I knew they had the ability if they could get the motivation. They had already demonstrated their capability to accomplish what seemed almost impossible. Abusers at every level demonstrate that uncanny ability to acquire essential materials to practice their abuse. The "desire to acquire" is a driving force that, if recycled into something positive, can empower radical change.

People who shared their garbage with me during classes and counseling sessions related diverse experiences, some of which were helpful to them but many were not. When asked, they readily admitted they learned valuable lessons from almost all those experiences. At that point, I challenged them to further analyze those lessons and apply them to life. For all of us, lessons learned while hauling garbage may be recycled and applied as a preventive to collecting it and as encouragement to getting rid of it.

Lessons learned from past mistakes are remarkably effective in destroying the "I'm no good" feeling for those who have it. An emphasis on recycling reaffirms the goodness in them and lets them become aware that they are not as sorry and hopeless as assumed. Affirmation of their ability to reason and to relate enables the recycling of other basic building blocks for further improvements. Recycling personal garbage is worth all the effort it requires.

Collecting and hauling garbage are hard work. Some of us exert excessive energy to get and keep our personal garbage. Apparently for some, there is little energy left after we collect and keep our garbage. We would have greater potential for a wholesome and happy life if only that energy could be recycled. It is reasonable to assume that the less effort and time we spend collecting and keeping garbage the more effort and time, we have to collect and keep what is productive. Anyone who thinks this is not an important issue needs only to work with heavy abusers and discover the time-consuming effort they exert in order to continue their use. Since they aren't the only people who exhaust themselves in misdirected efforts and misdeeds, there is a great need for recycling much of our energy.

Having done our best to properly dump and recycle our garbage, we may not yet be totally free from it. The effects of its previous presence may remain obvious, even after an honest attempt to clean the can. Garbage collected and carried for months and years etches its long-lasting imprint on the physical, emotional, and mental levels of our life. Some of those imprints may affect us forever because certain things cannot be undone and others cannot be redone.

Similar to a stinking household garbage can, our personal container may appear empty but the residue reminds us of what was there. This truth is not intended to discourage our upward journey but it is a reminder of another area with which we must be concerned. This statement does not suggest improvement and recovery are hopeless but it does point to a danger that must not be overlooked. Given the situation, what can we do? A possible and very practical solution is to "plant a rose" right in the middle of the mess. A prominent man, suffering from deep depression, sat in the midst of his multicolored rose garden. He noticed how beautiful and healthy the roses were, compared to the previous year. He wondered why. The only difference was, during the winter, he saturated the rose garden with manure. Obviously, his roses liked manure. They rewarded his efforts by providing pungent and pleasant odors that blocked the smell of manure, recycled its contents and lifted him from depression.

There is a lesson here for us. We need not permanently dwell on the problems caused by the residue of dumped and recycled garbage. We can put something in our life that is bigger and more powerful than it, i.e., "plant a rose" in its midst. Get involved in something that excites and challenges us to healthy and wholesome living. Become a dedicated parent and mate, get an advanced degree, develop a dormant talent, or any other possibility that offers advancement.

In short, do something that will dress up and cover up the remaining scars while adding new color and power to life. Having done that, the sweet smell of success will hopefully overshadow the residue of any remaining garbage. The residue may remain but its power is greatly diminished.

The seed of self- worth is the most important thing to plant in the residue. If this seed is not planted and if it does not grow, nothing else will produce positive results for very long. If the feeling of worthlessness continues, we will be propelled further into the garbage collecting business. Overly active garbage collectors will enter a new occupation only after they have sense of self-worth.

Frequently, it is foolish and futile to expect them to plant those seeds by themselves. For them, those seeds are extremely rare and they may not recognize one of them if they saw it. Furthermore, they probably would not plant it if they had one because they would not expect it to grow. Some competent outsider will likely have to help them prepare the seed bed, identify and plant the seed and nourish the tender plant during its infancy.

The growing plant's foliage and fruit gradually cover old maladies, add new flavor to life and transform the surroundings into a more pleasant place. Old garbage is recycled when new plants feed on it. The old scars are comfortably concealed by the new growth. What first seemed impossible becomes possible when the seed of self-worth begins to grow. If that plant withers and dies, one will return to big-time garbage collecting and recovery becomes even more difficult. The death of self-esteem reaffirms the "I'm no good feeling" and makes the soil far less receptive to any future planting of that seed.

Wise people avoid collecting unnecessary garbage. As simple as it sounds, this is an excellent strategy for life. It is surprising how many of us pay little or no attention to the source of our unwanted garbage but we complain vociferously about its presence. Those who avoid collecting it have fewer problems getting rid of it.

As usual, there is more than one way to accomplish this goal and each approach must be tailored to fit the individual. We reduce the likelihood of others placing unwanted garbage in our receptacle when we put a tight lid on it. There is so much garbage available and so few places to get rid of it that other people fill our can if we allow it. Some are very generous with their garbage and believe we deserve or want it. We sometimes unintentionally invite others to give us their garbage. An open and obvious receptacle invites others to fill it. Therefore, it is up to us to cover our can and make it more difficult for others to put unwanted garbage in it.

It is wise to learn from where you are getting unwanted garbage and make changes to avoid collecting it. If five beers with the boys every Friday night after work invariably causes a quarrelsome week-end with the wife, and you don't like it, perhaps you can come straight home after work and go out with the family.

If a weekly trip to see mama always sets you or your mate on edge, perhaps it is time to visit mama less frequently. If you have a habit of getting drunk or high when your finances run low, perhaps it is time to consume less and work smarter. Garbage doesn't just fall out of the sky. It has a definite source or cause that can usually be identified without great effort or expense. In order to uncover its source, carefully consider what you did, where you were, how you behaved, the pattern you followed, etc. Small and well-chosen changes in behavior and lifestyle may give gigantic rewards by purposefully putting you on a new road with much less available garbage.

There will be less room for garbage to collect and less likelihood of accidentally collecting it if we focus on doing what is constructive and productive. A life full of good and growing things has no need or room for excess garbage. Garbage has a habit of accumulating in and eventually filling the empty spaces. It is advisable for us to make an intelligent effort to carefully control what goes on in our life and to remain purposely, productively and pleasantly engaged. It is urgent for us to establish attainable goals, schedules and guidelines as a safeguard against empty space and unwise choices.

This point deserves special emphasis, particularly for those seeking recovery from extensive abuse. It is especially important to everyone who collected garbage for years and who recently began a new approach to life. Extra available hours and lack of plans are almost insurmountable problems for them to overcome.

Empty space in life is frightening and extremely dangerous. We want it filled instantly. Those attempting to turn away from what consumed them for so long, and lacking knowledge of what to do, are in an extremely vulnerable position. Knowing not what to do, they tend to do what they know.

Without competent encouragement and help, many of them will feel pain, fear the future and find temporary relief in their former lifestyle. Recovery is greatly facilitated when beginners are almost overrun by constructive things to do. There is no way to put anything into a full container unless something is first removed. In the final analysis, we are deliberately in the garbage collecting business, allowing it to collect in the empty spaces, or we purposefully fill all available space with constructive things.

Dirty old household garbage containers can be cleaned and restored for further use. Restoration may be more difficult for some. Old containers may never look as good as new but they are very usable in their restored state. Also, they are often superior to any possible replacement. Their dents and dings add character and indicate they are made of stern stuff. Similar statements can be truthfully made about people. At the core of our being, we are made of stern stuff. The dents and dings do not necessarily destroy us. They may indicate how strong we are, reflecting strengths instead of weakness. We do not necessarily need something new there. We only need to be cleaned, reshaped and restored. That wonderful possibility is available to everyone because we are human. Ridding ourselves of unnecessary garbage and restoring the receptacle are refreshing experiences and reflect the basic stuff of which we are made.

Dragging old and useless garbage wherever we go robs others and us of our power and purpose. Excessive garbage in others and us has a rippling effect. Therefore, our personal garbage is not totally personal after all. My garbage may affect you and yours has a tendency to affect me. Therefore, it behooves us to join forces, encouraging and enabling each other to be refreshed and renewed.

Those who have no knowledge that renewal is possible must be informed. Those who lack strength to begin the process must receive assistance. Those who made a feeble and failed attempt at recovery deserve another chance. Those who know how to successfully avoid collecting unnecessary garbage are encouraged to share their formula. Those who have the skills to appropriately dispose of their own garbage are urged to shepherd others in that process. Emptying the garbage is every one's business, in more ways than one.

We all have personal garbage. Each of us will continue to collect it as long as we live. Our life is inevitably affected by it. Our health and happiness are directly affected by our ability to properly dispose of it. Our collection of it will diminish and proper disposal will more likely occur through individual and collective efforts. Removal of the garbage refreshes and refurbishes our life and enhances renewal for others and ourselves. In order to have health and wholeness, each of us must consciously give some time and effort to trashing the trash.

CHAPTER 8

Dealing with Devils

New and intriguing ideas spring forth from unsuspected places. For many years I eagerly sought paradigms and models to explain and illustrate some human condition. My most desired models are those in which a person can easily see themselves and thereby gain insights not easily found or readily accepted from other sources.

Even though I am an ordained and professional clergyman, I had not found in the Bible a usable model specifically suited for abuse and recovery. To my surprise and delight, while reading the Bible for some other purpose, I accidentally discovered a profound model that was precisely what I sought. I read the passage many times before but never caught the connection, possible because of its brevity. It contains three short verses.

Even though written hundreds of years ago, it is as modern as the morning news. The short passage is in The Gospel of Matthew, chapter twelve, verse forty-three through forty-five (Matt. 12:43-45). A corresponding passage is located in The Gospel of Luke, chapter eleven, verse twenty-four through twenty-six (Luke 11:24- 26). Both passages are almost identical except Matthew adds a significant line. As I casually read the passage, new insights leaped from the page and almost overwhelmed me. I suddenly saw in this brief passage an analogy for human life, especially for those who practice any type of abusive behavior. Having seen it, I have a deeper understanding of addiction, abuse, deviant behavior and the serious difficulty in overcoming them. With some interpretation from me and some personal pondering, perhaps others will also catch the connection.

Modern translations of the passage speak of an "unclean spirit." Some translations refer to an "evil spirit" or "devil." The lesson of the passage is the same, regardless of which name we use. The story first appears to be very simple. For some unknown reason, an "unclean spirit" vacated a man or house. Perhaps it chose to look for something better but most likely it was thrown out.

Wandering in the desolate desert was no fun so the "devil" returned to its former dwelling place. Upon its return, the previous living quarters were empty, clean, orderly and unguarded. Being pleasantly surprised by what he found, the "unclean spirit" rushed out and persuaded seven of his close friends to move in with him.

The story can be easily told in pictorial form that may enhance our understanding of it. It is best viewed as three snapshots of a house or person, taken in sequence and separated by time.

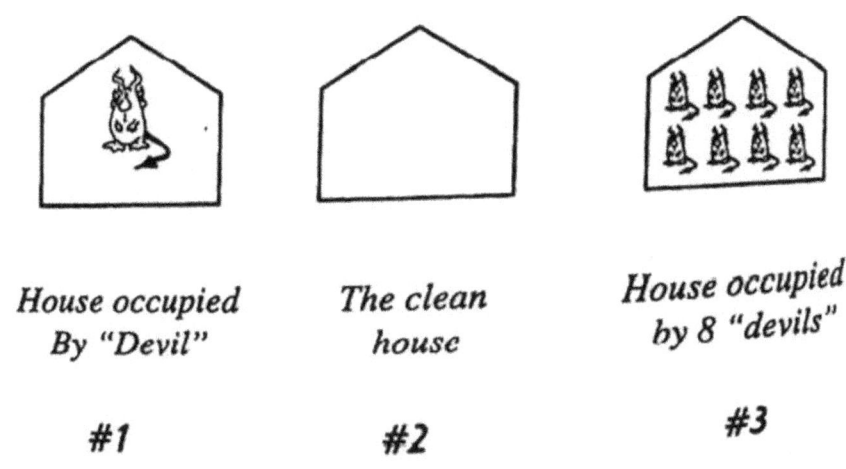

House occupied
By "Devil"

The clean
house

House occupied
by 8 "devils"

#1

#2

#3

The term "unclean spirit" or "devil" may cause us to read no further or deny the value of this illustration. An "unclean spirit," with independent power that allows it to think and move as it chooses, may disturb us. It behaves like a devil. The author of this passage may have had a different understanding of spirits than we but that need not cause us to disregard the passage. Even for him, it may be an excellent analogy of human experiences and not intended as a historical account.

If we accept no more than that, the passage has tremendous worth for us. If the matter of unclean spirits with independent and devilish power bothers us, we have much to learn about those suffering from any abuse, addiction and deviant behavior. Before we totally dismiss the idea of unclean spirits or devils with independent power, it is wise to listen carefully to those who suffer.

Heavy abusers frequently used almost identical terms to describe themselves and their behavior. They spoke of being unable to control themselves, of being overpowered even when they desired to act differently, as if some outside power made them do it. They inferred, "The devil made me do it," and many declared the same when they thought it was safe to do so. These people apparently experienced precisely what the above verses reflect. We may wish to skip this passage, not because we disbelieve in independent evil spirits but because it forces us to deal with fundamental issues in our life that it uncovers. Perhaps we do not want to examine the passage because we have also experienced it and are frightened by it. Come to think of it, we all know something about "evil spirits" and "devils" but are afraid to admit it.

The passage comes to life when we interpret the "unclean spirit" or "devil" as some undesirable behavior or character flaw. Since it exists in us, we, not it, decide it must go. Having made that decision, we undertake its expulsion through whatever means appear appropriate. Most who tried that approach discover the "devil" usually returned after a short time.

Unless we made radical changes during the elimination process, the "evil spirit" returned and we went back to our old tricks. It also returned with added power, often accompanied by its kin. Upon returning, it became more entrenched than before. It was much harder to throw out the second time because it got the best of us the first time. We tried to eliminate it but failed.

The reason we failed is unimportant at this juncture. The "evil spirit" won and we lost! It gained a foothold, a psychological advantage. We are threatened and frightened by it. Any attempt to eradicate it again will be less likely because we previously failed, and who wants to fail a second time? Indeed, the last condition is much worse than the first. It is obvious why we don't want to deal with "evil spirits" and "devils!"

An illustration may help clarify the point, if any clarification is needed. Smoking is hazardous to human health and requires expenditure of funds often needed for other important things. Suppose a smoker recognized the dangers and decided to quit cold turkey. He smoked his last cigarette and bought no more. He chewed more gum, drank more coffee, ate more rich food, gained more weight, etc., but did nothing to negate the need originally met by smoking. Likewise, he disregarded the power of addiction to nicotine. In short, he did nothing to guard against the return to smoking. Before much time elapsed, he smoked again. The "devil" returned.

Likewise, due to added weight, unhealthy eating habits, etc., his physical state may be worse than when he quit smoking cigarettes. The old behavior returned and any new attempt to quit will be far more difficult to initiate. As in the biblical passage, this condition is much worse than the first. We make this passage more inclusive and personal by giving the "evil spirit" or "devil" a name synonymous with any of our undesirable and unhealthy human behavior. The name may change but the principle and the results remain the same.

Those "evil spirits" in us deserve serious attention. They are present in us because we chose to provide them living space. Circumstances and situations influenced that choice but it was ours. We made our choice for some reason that made good sense to us at that time and under those conditions.

Time and time again, we recognize our kinship with the man who was walking down a sidewalk in a western city. He came upon a cactus garden and briefly paused to study it. He walked away, paused, turn around, rushed back to it, jerked off his clothes and jumped into the middle of the cactus. Instantly, he began to scream and call for help. Befuddled bystanders rushed to his aid and extricated him from the cactus. Hundreds of cactus barbs were embedded in his body and blood oozed from several places. A brave bystander asked, "Fellow, why in the world did you do that?" He thought for a moment and replied, "Right now I don't know, but at the time I did it I thought it was a good idea."

Even though we later learned that we chose to figuratively jump into the cactus patch, our choice was most likely made because it met some need, filled some painful void, made us feel good (or at least, less bad) and resolved an immediate problem. We learned what once met an immediate need or solved a particular problem eventually created more problems than it solved. Its kin came to live with it. That which we once deliberately chose slowly reduced our choices and now dramatically affects what we choose. That which once served us must now be served by us. Our other needs are not very important now because that is the nature of "evil spirits" and "devils." They dictate our choices and give us the bill to pay. We did not plan to become addicted but we are. We had not anticipated addiction's powerful sneak attack or its power to remain after we forcefully told it to go away. Our later state is worse, by far, than the first. The biblical passage is definitely correct.

"Evil spirits" came to dwell in our house, i.e., in us, because we unknowingly and unintentionally invited them. Thinking they were something else, we may have welcomed them! They will not leave on their own volition nor will they leave when politely asked. They will not depart until we consciously decide they must go and until we muster the strength to force them out.

Once removed, they will not stay out unless we purposefully guard against their return. Our choices gave them quarters and only our choices will make them homeless. There is no other way to displace them. Our "evil spirit," our private "devil," cannot be expelled by concerned parents, a loving mate, a close friend, the staff of a treatment center or a stronger "evil spirit."

Competent and concerned persons can only help us at certain points. Without them helping us, we are much more likely to fail. However, we must each make the crucial choices, fight the fiercest battles, and endure the agony of our private world. Others are needed to point the way for us, provide competent help and accompany us on the journey. The pivotal point, the decision to expel the undesirables and to keep them out, is always ours to make. No one can make it for us. Unless that decision is ours alone the "evil spirits" will not be permanently removed.

The above-mentioned biblical passage provides a framework for further insights. By borrowing the basic components of its story, we can tell it again but make some changes. The changed story can also be portrayed in pictorial form. As in the previous pictorial representation, we use three separate snapshots of the same house or person, taken in sequence and with the passage of time between them.

"Devil" in the house.

\# 1

A clean house with a "Devil" at the door.

#2

A full house with a "Devil" at the door.

#3

The first snapshot depicts an "evil spirit" well established, unpacked and settled in. There it intends to remain, and will, unless the owner forces it out. There it intends to remain, and will, unless the owner forces it out. The second snapshot was taken some time after the first. During that time the owner decided to expel the unwanted intruder and managed to do so by using whatever means and efforts necessary. He may have done it primarily alone or he may have had the help of others.

The second snapshot deserves careful attention because it reflects fundamental facts that must be forever remembered. Even though it was expelled, the "evil spirit" did not disappear or go in search of another abode. It did not even move away from the front door through which it was thrown.

The "devil" defiantly stands with its foot firmly against the door, checking to see if the door was accidentally unlocked or poorly fastened. It will patiently wait and watch for any indication that reentry is possible, either through the door or any other unguarded opening. It seeks to reenter in its old form but if denied, it will disguise itself in another tempting form. If the owner of the house must open the door for other things, he must remember it is there, forcefully fling it aside, demand its departure, and secure the door. Even though forced from the house, most "evil spirits" will never move far from the front door.

The third snapshot reflects the ideal way to keep "unclean spirits" out of a clean house, even though they may constantly lurk outside. A sure way to keep undesirable things out of a house is to first fill it with desirable and necessary things and then insure it remains full. Once the house has been deliberately filled with constructive and productive things there will be no room or need for the undesirable "devils." Even though "evil spirits" remain outside the house, we have no need to panic. That is where we want them to stay.

We are reasonably safe as long as we are aware of their presence, maintain our commitment to keep them out, and keep the house full of top-quality things. Vicious "devils" have always been and will continue to prowl outside our door. Primary attention must be given to keeping the house full of desirable things and not to the "devils" lurking outside. Focusing our attention on what is or may be outside robs us of our ability to nurture, refine, replace and enjoy the high value items within. Once again, we always give attention and respond to whatever we value most.

Each snapshot in the second set above tells its own story. Put all three of them together as one picture and they form a provocative model. The model portrays a process easily understood and discussed but much more difficult to follow. The model they create depicts in pictorial form the recovery process from any abuse, addiction and deviant behavior. Recovery, or getting rid of an "evil spirit," is far more likely to begin after we understands the process and pinpoints our position in it. This model facilitates both. No stretch of the imagination or superior intelligence is required to substitute appropriate words into the model. Substitute the name of any abuse, addiction, deviant behavior, unhealthy habit, etc., in the place of "evil spirit" and the process and principle remain the same. The model provides the means to identify where we are in the recovery process and offers a way to measure our progress on the road to recovery. It also points to some stumbling blocks and suggests helpful behavior.

The first pictorial presentation of the biblical passage, the first set of three pictures, depicts abuse and addiction. The second set of three pictures with interpretations depicts the recovery process. Combine both sets of pictures into one large model and it is simple enough to be understood by most and unique enough to be refreshing. During an earlier discussion of the recovery process, I gave great importance to having our life adequately and properly filled. As suggested earlier, the ideal way to remain free from harmful habits and behavior, "evil spirits," is to be fully involved in wholesome living. That point cannot be over emphasized. It demands and deserves further emphasis. Old habits and harmful behavior often fill a large portion of one's life, especially those who seriously need renewal for any reason.

When those items are removed, or are in the process of being removed, empty spaces appear. That vacant space poses serious problems because it will not remain vacant very long. Something new will fill the spot or the old will return with greater power, as illustrated in the biblical passage mentioned above. Herein lies one of the greatest stumbling blocks to recovery because it is either unknown or overlooked by those who hurt as well as those who seek to help. Persons in the initial stage of recovery are extremely vulnerable to anything that looks promising. Their lack of information an exuberant desire to change emphasize their need for competent help. They know the goal but they need some helpful guidelines to reach it. They desperately need some criteria by which to judge any suggested substitutes that might fill the empty spaces in their life.

For many reasons, it is impossible for one person to identify every suitable substitute that may be useful to anyone seeking recovery. The best we can do is offer guidelines, or criteria, by which a person can evaluate and judge any available choice to fill the void. These guidelines must be general enough to include every person and possibility but specific enough to point a person in the proper direction. From that perspective, the following criteria were selected.

Wise and helpful space fillers are constructive and productive. This is extremely vague but it is a valid point at which to start. Most people have some comprehension of what it means. With thoughtful effort, they will be able to use it as a judging device. It advocates avoiding anything destructive to them and others. It suggests that we think before we act. It means that we know where we intend to go and have some idea of how we might get there. This is a gigantic move in the proper direction, especially since much of the former lifestyle was destructive to someone.

Most people know something is productive when it contributes to what is good for themselves and others. It means we are doing something other than standing still or moving backward. We are moving toward a predetermined goal. When the goal is recovery and properly filled spaces in our lives, anything that does no harm and moves us toward that goal holds great promise.

We have a second criterion for judging any possible space filler. It should contribute toward health and wholeness. These words are also vague but they offer some help. In most cases, if not all, our major malady is best described as a sickness and our primary need is health or wholeness. In order to be healed, the pain must at least be reduced if not eradicated. Every abuser has some idea of what he or she is doing to cause some of their pain. If we do not precisely know what the primary pain is and what causes it, we need to know immediately.

Any possible addition that soothes the present pain, eliminates its cause and does no harm to others and us appears to be a valid choice. Anything that moves us toward becoming a complete person who is positively connected to the whole human race offers tremendous possibilities. Cautious trial and error, coupled with instant evaluation, will enable each person to identify helpful items. Consultation with competent counselors can be very fruitful.

Whatever we add to our life should make us feel good. Having said that, a word of caution must be added. This is not the popular adage, "If it feels good, do it." However, if it consistently fails to give us "a good feeling" we will soon cease to do it. Let us remember there is a serious distinction between instant gratification and lasting pleasure. The latter is far more valuable than the former but the first should not be avoided simply because it is short lived. Each must be measured by its harmless, positive, productive and long range effect.

Momentary pleasures that do no harm are much better than no pleasures. Likewise, temporary and fleeting "good feelings" are not worth the time and effort required if they ultimately are more detrimental than beneficial. Let us also remember that laughter and genuine pleasure are not necessarily synonymous.

Genuine pleasure may not make us laugh but it sure makes us feel good deep inside. We desperately need to feel good but it is much more important to feel good about ourselves. The latter will be an elixir for our pain and an impetus for our recovery. Chemically induced feelings and other abusive behavior are seldom "good," even though they frequently make one temporarily feel less bad.

Since consumed chemicals diminish a person's awareness of reality, perhaps the "good feelings" they reportedly produce are more imaginary than real, more a dream than reality, more camouflage than cure, and certainly more temporary than permanent. We should be skeptical of anything that regularly makes us irrational, ill, irritable or its slave. It seldom contributes anything toward feeling good, physically or emotionally.

Abusive behavior probably originates from an attempt to feel good, or less bad, but it does not make one feel good about themselves. Likewise, it does not make others feel good and lacks any signs of genuine goodness. A brief period of feeling less bad has some value but should not be confused with feeling good about ourselves. We need to deliberately fill space in our lives with what makes us feel good, but especially with what makes others and us feel good about ourselves.

We should deliberately choose each item selected to fill space and enhance our recovery. This matter is too important to pick blindly something from a hat or to let another choose for us. Well-meaning multitudes freely and forcefully tell us what should be added, even though they know little or nothing about our need. Since they don't understand us and are also unqualified gurus, we do well to disregard many of their suggestions. There is a more important reason to turn a deaf ear to them. Happiness, health and wholeness depend upon making our own choices. Immeasurable misery is often generated when someone forces a choice on others.

Those who forced their choice on another may have meant well but it never seems to turn out well. Recipients of coerced choices frequently become unhappy and unhealthy people. Those who were coerced to attend a particular educational institution, major in a prescribed subject, accept a certain occupation, have a particular type wedding service, live in a designated place, etc., often engage in unhealthy things to compensate for their inner pain. We wholeheartedly agree with and accept the choice for our own or else it will eventually come back to bite us. Given all this, we still need helpful suggestions, possible alternatives, counsel and advice but we do not need someone to choose for us.

Every item we choose to fill space in our life needs to fit into a well-made and long-range plan. Choices with good potential will surely fail when they have no supporting cast. Definite plans have value beyond themselves. They indicate intent, hope, commitment, thought, etc., all of which are positive signs for recovery.

Extensive plans that go in opposite directions waste time and effort. Incongruent plans confuse the issues and the person to such an extent recovery is thwarted, if not lost. Short-range plans are also necessary but they serve best when dovetailed into a much bigger plan. If my goal is continued sobriety, it is very unwise for me to accept a last-minute invitation to spend the night out with the boys who still drink. Such short-range behavior is not helpful in maintaining the long-term goal of sobriety.

A five-year plan for saving money to make the down payment on a house will not happen if there is deficit spending each and every month. Short-range plans do not necessarily have to provide astronomical support for a long-range plan but it is wise to avoid anything that detracts from or interferes with the predetermined goal. Plans for simple and temporary things may be very beneficial. Plans, both long-range and short-range, are intended to facilitate primary control of our lives, when and where possible. Plans help us make things happen.

These suggested guidelines for selecting suitable substance to fill the void spots in our life have additional strength when used as a group. No single guideline is strong enough to weed out every possible unwise choice. When all of them, and others that may surface, are individually applied to a possible choice and that possible choice passes the test, it is worthy of tentative acceptance.

An amazing amount of time is unexpectedly available to a person who recently ceased to "use and abuse." Former "devils" occupied an extensive amount of space in unsuspected places. Numerous persons in rehabilitation and recovery have given no thought to and made no plans for using that extra and unfilled space. Recidivism is much more likely for those who are not aware of its danger and who do not deliberately seek healthy ways to fill it. "Unclean spirits" love that situation and thrive on it. Since spare space has been largely disregarded during rehabilitation and since it is crucial to recovery, the above general guidelines for filling that space may need enhancement with some specific suggestions.

Any person entering recovery is implored to associate with a professional support group that specializes in their problem area. Alcoholics Anonymous (A.A.) and Narcotics Anonymous (N.A.) are two such groups, but there are others. Support groups of this type have helped thousands kick the habit and remain clean, soberand free from abuse. There are no other sources that offer as much as they in their respective field. A word of caution is in order for anyone attending the first group meeting. Groups, like people, have individual quirks and idiosyncrasies because they are composed and maintained by people. If you stumble into one that does not meet your need, quickly look for another. Whatever you do, don't give up on going to such meetings.

Also, be prepared for some painful moments because the members have been where you are and they will not allow you to offer flimsy excuses or play mind games with them. Honesty is a key to full participation in a support group. Be honest with yourself, even if you choose to look for another group. There is a group near you that is capable of helping you recover. There is normally no shortage of support groups but if there is, start one with a few others who have a similar malady. Active participation in one or more of these groups can fill more free time than one has to give.

Users and abusers have family fences that desperately need mending. Extended abuse invariably and adversely affects family members. Even though only one member may have practiced abuse, the family unit most often became sick. Conversely, it is also possible that a sick family unit contributed to individual members becoming abusive. Even when some family members are not seriously sick, there are obvious and hidden problems that must be resolved before the family is restored to a functional relationship. Deeply divided families may require professional counseling in order to recover, if recovery is possible. Even if the immediate family unit cannot be fully restored, some constructive resolution must be reached.

There are other extended family relationships that must be mended and maintained before healing and health can come to the abuser. Abuse drove a wedge between family members and they drifted apart. It will take time and talk for them to find each other and unite again. There are almost endless possibilities for restoring family relationships. Spending quality time together is an excellent place to start. Simple and enjoyable togetherness opens doors to far reaching possibilities, many of which could not be attained otherwise. Honest feelings that are shared and encouraged may reduce the distance that divides.

All members deserve a chance to state their needs and desires. Reading self-help books and following outlined exercises unite family members in constructive activities. Family counseling may facilitate rapid recovery. Remember and revive old activities that once meant so much to the family. Give inexpensive or handmade gifts to family members when there is no special occasion.

Family members want the abuser to show some signs that recovery is real, especially if their hopes were dashed on another occasion. Genuine concern for and quality time spent with the family may provide the sign they seek. There are more ways to spend quality time with the family than anyone can exhaust.

A person entering recovery needs a responsible and good job, either because they lost the one they had or to enhance self-worth. For many, poor performances, prolonged absences, and paltry excuses produced their inevitable reward. Let us remember that people lose responsible jobs in both paid and unpaid positions. For all practical purposes, one may forfeit their position as trusted mate, loving father or mother, dependable person, etc. Abuse exacts a high price.

For those who were gainfully employed, the price often includes unemployment and numerous unpaid bills. After extended abuse, one's financial burden may be so great that they need to work twenty-four hours a day and seven days a week in order to catch up. Finding a responsible and financially rewarding job facilitates self-esteem but the urgent need for income and the availability of employment can create additional difficulties.

If one is employed, a second job or extended hours are advisable only if they solve more problems than they create. For the unemployed, meaningful and high paying jobs may be hard to find, especially if a person was fired or quit their previous one. Therefore, relocation or retraining may be advisable in order to get a new job, but that may encompass other dangers.

Finding a new job or restoring meaning and purpose to an old one will not happen overnight. Large blocks of time can be consumed in preparation for a new job or in getting up to speed in the one you have. Persons in recovery can wisely spend an enormous amount of time looking for a good job, working on the job and improving their skills for either.

Acquiring additional education is an excellent way to fill time, either for short or extended periods. Seeking additional education not only fills time but it has other wonderful advantages. It opens doors to personal enrichment, a new career, a larger salary, relocation, association with different people, etc.

Pursuing education just for the sake of learning is a wonderful luxury few of us will ever have. If it is pursued in conjunction with other vital concerns, there is almost no limit to the amount of time one could spend in that endeavor. Educational pursuits need not be limited to a college classroom or a degree program. On-the- job training, personal research, apprenticeships, correspondences courses, self-help courses, etc., may be more readily available and more advantageous to some, especially when formal education is not available or affordable. Everyone can enhance health, happiness and wholeness through education but it takes time. Those entering recovery may have more free time at that point in their life than they will ever have again.

Making and managing a budget demands immediate attention from those entering recovery from serious abuse or addiction and will consume large blocks of time. Some will have little money and large debts. Much too late they learned, "When your out-go is more than your income then your upkeep will be your downfall." In order to prevent even further deterioration in their financial condition, a strict budget and a workable financial plan must be instituted immediately.

Every available penny must be put to maximum use in order to remain financially afloat. Face to face negotiation with creditors is essential and they want more than warmed over promises or new excuses. Arrangements for delayed payments or an adjusted schedule for payments may be necessary. Honesty with the creditors does not pay off the debts but it is one of the wiser ways of buying additional time to pay them. When and where possible, performing good deeds and odd jobs make favorable impressions that may convince the creditor, and others, recovery is underway.

Managing money during recovery from serious abuse and addiction frequently poses two severe problems. Lack of money is the first. Numerous people enter recovery with a multitude of unpaid bills that plague them and the entire family. Deleting that debt seems almost insurmountable. When a measly amount of money becomes available, it will not make a dent in the giant debt. Furthermore, where is it most advantageous to apply the paltry amount?

At this juncture, a strong temptation arises to forget the bills and spend the few available dollars on old habits, thereby briefly having a good time and forgetting financial woes. The "unclean spirit" lurks at the door! That temptation overcomes many with excellent intentions. Realistic plans, an awareness that the strong temptation will come and competent outside encouragement help avoid this ever-present pitfall.

The second severe financial problem is opposite the first. If those in recovery have a few dollars that are not demanded elsewhere, they may not know what to do with them. During the days of abuse and addiction, the amount of dollars in the pocket frequently determined the amount of use. Old habits are hard to break, especially when they existed for years. The "devil" remains near the door!

The compelling temptation is to spend immediately those extra dollars and spend them where numerous others were spent, for drugs and drink or whatever. The "devil" waits patiently by the door for any opportunity or excuse to enter again! Excess dollars in the pocket can be a devastating thing when there is no meaningful plan to put them to constructive use. Persons in recovery should carefully make and faithfully follow a realistic financial plan. Failure to do so unlocks the door to that "evil spirit" of recidivism.

Persons in recovery need to devote some time to recreational activities. Abuse often leads to atrophy of the muscles and the mind. Proper exercise works wonders for the body and the brain. It offers another chance and reason to do something you wanted to do but never got around to doing it. When properly done, it is good therapy and not a waste of time or money. Selected activities will be more frequent, more prolonged and more productive when they encompass enjoyable items that stretch the mind and body. Hobbies are included in this category.

Complicated and extensive programs are helpful for some but not necessary for everyone. Inexpensive activities that excite the mind and renew the body are adequate. The key is not what we do but its contribution to health, happiness and wholeness. Recreation is medicine for the mind, soul and body. Each of us must find the time to take our preventive medicine if we want to gain and maintain our health.

Anyone looking for a place to constructively spend time need not look further than the nearest social services agency. Apparently, every one of them needs more volunteers than they get. They come in various sizes and types and are designed to meet specific problems encountered by diverse people. Some cater to the young, some to the old and others to anyone in need of what they offer. There is a place of service for almost anyone who is willing to volunteer time and talent.

Specific skills and physical dexterity are desirable but there is an abundant need for someone to be physically present for another. Some agencies provide opportunities for volunteers to share lessons learned from abuse and in recovery. The youth and disadvantaged tend to listen to those in recovery because the speaker's scars validate their story and their story resonates with the listener's experience.

Volunteer service for others offers a chance to atone for previously wasted time and is a wonderful way to use any available free time. For at least two reasons, giving to others may be far more important than we had assumed. First, giving to others may be the only way to truly keep what we have. As strange as it may sound, that is true for some of the best things in life, because, if kept only for oneself, they smother and die. Second, upon departing this life, we may take with us only that which we graciously gave away. That also seems impossible but it is one of the strange things about human existence. If we cannot take it with us, perhaps we can send it ahead!

I know of no better place to spend time than in a church or synagogue of our choice. No other organization offers more than they. An A.A. or N.A. group runs a close second because, in some sense, they are very similar and meet many of the same basic needs.

Churches and synagogues epitomize what is most needed by a person entering recovery. They proclaim and practice forgiveness, acceptance, support, guidance, and unconditional love. They provide a place to begin again, opportunities to be with other struggling souls, and a point to connect with the eternal.

Some faith groups are more closely attuned to this basic purpose and others may not offer what a newcomer expects. Since they encompass other humans, don't expect them to be perfect. If you are dissatisfied with what you find, immediately go to another group.

Ask friends, neighbors, and fellow support group members for suggestions or visit for personal knowledge. Churches and synagogues normally have a wide variety of helpful activities. We must choose whatever holds the greater promise for desired help and whatever our available time allows. One participates not only to receive what is offered but also to give for the betterment of others. There are enough opportunities for receiving and giving to fill all the free time anyone has.

No person has any reason to complain about idle time or the unavailability of something constructive to do. We have more accessible places to spend available time wisely than we have time to spend.

However, there is another pertinent point worth noting. If those who are entering recovery spend all their recently acquired free time in only one positive area, they likely will not recover. That area can become their "god." Wise persons recognize there are many areas to which they must devote some time.

More power for recovery is generated and time is more productive when areas are combined. Recreational outings and volunteer work are ideal for family participation. Building and following a budget is a family affair. Job and additional education often overlap and both involve the family. Family participation in religious activities helps unite the family, provides educational and recreational opportunities, and could open the door to a new job. Wise and healthy persons move from one area to another as time and need suggest. They allocate their time, use it wisely, and seldom complain because they have too much.

New and meaningful models offer an opportunity to redesign our life so that we may more easily move toward healing and wholeness. A brief biblical passage provides us a new model worthy of serious consideration. It speaks to our human condition and offers a new guide for living. It points to possible "unclean spirits" in us and provides clues for dealing with "devils."

CHAPTER 9

Trusting the Truth

Dr. William Glasser presented a different approach to healing in a new book entitled Reality Therapy, published by Harper and Row in 1965. Ideas generated by his intriguing book struck a responsive cord with me. Perhaps it spoke to me because I am not impressed with imaginary friends, games of let's pretend, absolutely impossible dreams, practice preaching classes, and abstract art. Perhaps some people may interpret this as a personal flaw but I consider it an indicator of strength. I want reality with all its beautiful or ugly truth exposed so that I may examine it and appropriately respond. If I understand what he said, Dr. Glasser addresses the urgent necessity for us to seek and follow truth if we want health and wholeness. I believe his idea is extremely relevant for everyone seeking recovery of any kind. Regardless of who we are, truth is a significant guidepost on the road to recovery.

The term "reality therapy" need not frighten us. Every one of us would probably profit from and be delighted by appropriate therapy. "Reality therapy" is a specific type of therapy easily understood if we examine each word separately. Let us first look at "therapy."

In its broadest sense, it is anything that adds healing and wholeness to a person's existence. It helps heal or cure whatever ails us. In that sense, it may range from taking a daily noonday nap in the recliner to regularly scheduled sessions on a psychiatrist's couch. It may range from testing your mental skills in a trivial pursuit game to having your mental health tested through psychoanalysis. It may simply consist of sitting on the creek bank with a fishing pole in your hand or having special treatment done on a broken hand. Good therapy eventually makes us feel better. Nonprofessionals or highly trained specialist provide it. We provide it for others or ourselves. Its sources are abundant and readily available.

The word "reality" is also easily understood. It focuses on truth, not wishes or make believe. It is primarily concerned with what is, not with what might be or could have been. Like TV's Cop Joe Friday, it is concerned with the facts. It does not sugarcoat or camouflage. It uses no superfluous words or phrases to describe something. It calls a spade "a spade" and not a long-handled device that may be used for digging in the ground. For our purposes, it deals with the truth in our world where we live.

The foregoing and following comments are no attempt to define, describe or summarize Dr. Glasser's theory. He may disagree with what I am about to say but I am indebted to him for stimulating my thoughts on this subject. If I over simplify or misrepresent his theory, I trust I at least offer some therapy to people who need it.

In discussing "reality therapy," Dr. Glasser emphasizes the fact that each of us is responsible for who or what we are. It apparently follows that each must also accept the responsibility for making changes that move us toward health and wholeness. We discover reality as we discover truth, or vice versa. We cannot have one without the other. Given our human nature, recovery can come only by following and trusting the truth.

Genuine therapy of this type is greatly enhanced by each of us asking and answering two specific questions. The two encompassing questions must be kept in the proper order or the entire process will be useless. The first question must be asked and fully answered before it is appropriate to ask or seek answers to the second. The second question has no meaning or usefulness if asked and answered before the first. Finding honest answers to the questions is no easy task.

Many hours of serious thought are required to adequately answer them. They cannot be sensibly answered in one sitting or even in one day. It takes weeks or months to fully answer them. The answers are useless if they are not true, or as near the truth as we can get. After some time and additional insight, a number of initially selected answers will prove to be incorrect and will require replacement. Others will be correct but incomplete. Still others will need refinement and polish. Answering these questions is a tedious and time-consuming task that must not be refused or compromised if recovery is desired.

The first question must be asked about dozens of different things present in our life and in us. It is always a variation and continuation of, "What is?" What is going on in my life at this time? What is the situation, condition or circumstance with which I am presently confronted? What is the truth about me; my relationships with others; my financial condition; my job; my health; my education; my usual response to pressure and pain; the way I feel about myself, etc. Every subject affecting how I think and act needs to be covered. Honest and complete answers are essential for every topic.

Keep foremost in mind that we are searching for reality and truth. Finding and admitting reality will be time consuming and possibly painful because some truth is hidden and some hurts. If my family is dysfunctional, there is no healing value in pretending all is well within it. If I have only ten dollars, there is no help in pretending I can pay cash for a new Mercedes. If I am an abuser or addict, I will never get on the road to recovery unless I admit the truth about myself.

Honest answers will include virtues as well as vices. Some of us have problems saying positive things about ourselves because the "I'm no good devil" lives within or lurks just outside the door. Every person has some good qualities in them, regardless of who we are or what we have been. In order to be truthful about ourselves, we must also include the positive as well as the negative. If it is true, list it. Our personal goodness may be covered with trash and it may take some time to find it but it is there.

A certain man was well known for a particular trait. He habitually made a positive comment when viewing the remains of a deceased person during the funeral. Locals attended funerals just to see what he would say about the deceased. A reprobate also lived in that community. Upon his death, numerous people came from miles away to his funeral. They wanted to see if the kind gentleman could say something positive about the reprobate. At the appropriate time, the kind gentleman paused in front of the open casket and viewed the remains. The people waited in hushed silence and strained to hear him. He stared momentarily at the remains, looked out at the audience and said in voice audible to all, "Old Zeb sure could whistle well," and walked away.

I reiterate. Everyone has some good in them. It is untrue and unhealthy to believe otherwise. Restating the issue may better emphasize the good in us. My doctor may call me fat but I like to put a positive spin on it by saying I am very adept at keeping good food from spoiling. I can keep a large quantity of food from going to "waste" but it may go to "waist!"

One may be called careless with money but perhaps they want to provide instant and meaningful gratification for a terminally ill family member. One may be called unappreciative when they refuse a promotion on the job but they may not want to give up precious time or an ideal situation for the family. One may be called stingy when they do not wear the latest designer clothing but they may be providing clothes for the needy. Many negative traits have a corresponding positive trait. Likewise, viewed from a different perspective, they may be less negative than first thought. List whatever is true.

Appropriately answering the first major question mentioned above requires a systematic approach to "What is?" Any workable system is satisfactory, depending upon the complexity of the question and issue under consideration. Simple questions and issues need not be complicated with a complex process. I propose a system requiring several sheets of paper with a separate topic written on the top of each. Suggested topics and questions were previously given but there are many more necessary ones. Ponder a specific item under the sub-question and identify the truth in reference to that specific topic.

Write honest responses on the appropriately titled page. As an example, ask such questions as, "What is my financial status?" or "What is the health of my marriage?" etc. Put the recorded answers aside while you work on another topic. Reconsider the issue at a later time and add other answers or refine what was previously written. It is extremely helpful to keep pen and paper readily available at all times, even when you are not consciously working on the project. Answers will appear when least expected. They tend to get lost forever if they aren't instantly recorded. I speak from experience.

One night, just prior to drifting off to sleep, a wonderfully intriguing sermon idea raced unexpectedly through my mind. After pondering it for a few moments, I considered getting out of bed and writing it on the paper kept in a drawer by my bed for such a purpose. I eventually concluded that was useless because it was so enticing. Without further thought or delay, I went to sleep.

When I awoke the following morning, I immediately reached for a pen and paper to record the wonderful idea. The idea was no longer there. It escaped while I slept. To my knowledge, it never returned. Answers to individual parts of the first question are too important to lose. Every possible one should be carefully coddled, cuddled and recorded. Any one of them may hold the key that unlocks doors to a deeper understanding or it may be the grain of sand that overpowers denial.

Read and rewrite these answers until they become as inclusive and truthful as possible. Once every subject is carefully covered and completed, you have a poignant word picture describing in some measure who you believe you are, or "what is." Having asked and answered, "What is the truth for me?" in every possible area, the next suggested step is risky and may not be wise for everyone.

If you have a loving mate, dear friend or competent counselor whom you completely trust, and if you are able to endure the added pressure, share your answers with them. You share not for their approval or disapproval but for additional suggestions you may have overlooked. Add their suggestions only after you ponder them and are fully convinced, they are true. Their suggestions may help you polish some of your answers or add new ones.

Having labored long and carefully to find honest and complete answers for the first major question, we move to the second. It follows hard on the heels of the first. The first question asks, "What is?" The second continues by saying, "If that's what is, what do I want to do about it?" It is obvious why the first question must be fully and truthfully answered before any serious attention can be given to the second.

These two questions must always arise in the same order, whether a person is wrestling with a life size issue or with one of less proportion, if there is one. We must honestly answer the first before we can wisely answer the second. Our answer to the second question basically determines all we are and do. I cannot over emphasize the importance of seriously and honestly answering both questions. Honest answers to both, and in the proper order, are an absolute necessity for recovery, growth and wholeness.

The second question contains several specifics that deserve special attention. For emphasis, I repeat that it is predicated on the first, uses answers from the first question as a launching pad to answer it, and that the effectiveness of its answers depends on the honesty of the first answer. Special and extensive attention must be given to who responds to the second question. The "I" cannot be over emphasized. The second question is not concerned with what a mate, friend, parent or organization wants me to do. It does not ask what they will do about it. The question places the responsibility squarely on the individual who must decide. It is "I" who must do what "I" want with "what is" or the process is doomed. I must honestly respond to "what is" so that I may decide what I want.

We now recognize why we must honestly and personally answer the first question. Recovery and growth will not follow if my answers to either question resulted from bribery, trickery, theft or coercion. Truth is put to the test again because the course of action must be my choice and must reflect what I want. Individualism is not glorified here nor does it run roughshod over others. I made choices that brought me where I am in my life. I must assume responsibility for them and for what I choose to do about them. Recovery and wholeness demand nothing less.

Emphasis on the "I" encompasses far more than we may initially imagine. It presupposes the ability to do something and to do something constructive. Persons who see themselves as "no good" desperately need to know that there is hope for them. This emphasis on the "I" tells them they are responsible for what happens, good or bad, and opens the door to constructive change. It encourages positive action and allows a person freedom to act in whatever way is comfortable and deemed helpful to them at that moment in time.

It gently encourages them to first do simple things and accept greater responsibility when they are able.

By its very nature, the second question is no put-down nor does it insult or injure those with low self-esteem. The question equates them with the rest of the human race by quietly affirming that they can do something constructive and they are responsible, just like every other person. Many who suffer from low self- esteem do so because others have repeated declared or insinuated, they lack ability to choose or act wisely. The second question quietly undercuts excuses for inactivity and puts responsibility on each of us. Even though those with low self-esteem seriously answer this question, total rejuvenation isn't guaranteed. Their self-esteem may be so low that they need help to honestly answer it. Recovery depends on other helpful things but this is an excellent place to start.

Some of us acquired personal responsibility rather early in life while others delayed much too long. Some of us received it as a gift while others reached out and took it. At about age eleven, I was riding my red wagon on the front porch of my childhood home. The house had a long hallway that extended from the front porch toward the back of the house and ended as it opened out into the dining room. My parents were at the dining room table. Mom yelled down the hall, "You be careful out there or you'll run off that porch and break your neck."

She meant well, I'm sure, but I didn't like the insinuations she made. It sounded as if she really said, " You don't have sense enough to stay away from danger so I am assuming responsibility for your choices."

I don't know why she said that. I had ridden the wagon on the porch many times and never once ran off the edge or gotten hurt. I often went alone to the far fields on the farm and worked. I was a responsible lad with a level head. When she said that, something snapped in my mind. Perhaps I thought, "There are times when mothers would be more helpful if they were seen and not heard."

I rode back and forth across the porch a few times as I plotted my next move. Even though she had not intended to do so, Mom gave me an idea. I got out of my wagon near the swing, took hold of the tongue, pulled the wagon to the other end of the porch, leaped into the yard, pulled the wagon behind me, took the tongue and repeatedly banged the wagon on the ground and pretended to cry as if I were seriously injured.

Both parents rushed to my rescue. My father flung open the screen door with such force it slammed hard against the back wall. My mother was close behind him. When they reached the porch, I was standing on the ground a few feet from the door,

bursting with laughter. I didn't laugh for long! My father applied the board of education to the seat of knowledge and my backside burned for quite some time. Even though my prank proved to be painful, it was worth all the discomfort it caused. By my deliberately chosen action, I declared my personal responsibility for and ability to protect myself. I decided what I wanted to do about Mom's unnecessary comment.

The second question presupposes not only the ability to plan but also that a plan is forthcoming. This may be subtle but it is very significant because it gently encourages everyone to get moving, especially persons with low self-esteem. Due to certain circumstances, some people's ability to formulate plans may be at very low tide.

Some may require repeated encouragement, specific examples of their previous plans, and suggested possibilities before they recognize their ability to plan again. However, anyone who encourages and helps another must do nothing to indicate inability or to take away responsibility from the one who must choose.

Effective plans are not easily or quickly made, especially if they include long-range goals that involve other people. Effort and time are required to make and mesh short-range and long- range plans. We cannot safely neglect short or long-range plans because the lack or inappropriateness of either one thwarts growth and recovery.

My father lacked formal education but he was a wise man who illustrated for me the necessity to make and mesh short- range and long-range plans. Our farm was not flat land, so terraces were necessary to prevent erosion. Even as a young lad, I spent many hours helping my father build terraces.

To locate the exact position for a terrace, we used a simple   device he made. It consisted of a small straight board about twelve feet long. A short board was fastened at a right angle to each end of the long board as legs of equal length. Brackets in the middle of the long board held a regular carpenter's level. Having decided the general location where a terrace was needed, my father placed one leg of the device at the outer edge of the field and the other in the field. He moved the leg in the field until it was situated at a point on the ground slightly higher than the other, so that water would flow from the field to the outside. When the proper spot was located, he slid the legs back and forth on the ground to mark their place.

He then moved farther out into the field, the length of the board, and placed one leg in the previous mark farthest from the edge of the field. He again located the almost level spot and marked it. He repeated the process until he reached the other side of the field. About midway of the field he made the opposite end of the device slightly lower so the water would flow from the center of the field toward the other side and not all in one direction. I accurately mounded dirt over the mark after the device was moved to the next location. Small mounds of dirt correctly marked the crooked and almost level path across the field. My father took a plow and sequentially connected those mounds with a furrow. Repeated furrows created a terrace.

The illustrated lessons are obvious. My dad's long-range goal was a terrace in his field to control erosion. The identity of the almost level spots located twelve feet apart was his short-range goal. To successfully accomplish his long-range goal, i.e., build a usable terrace, it was absolutely necessary for him to meet each short-range goal by sequentially connecting each mound of dirt to the next with a furrow.

He could have connected only half of the mounds of dirt and several short-range goals would have been met but he would have no terrace to guard against erosion. He could have made a terrace without marking any intermediate points, by disregarding one marked point, or by adding a point outside the line but erosion would have destroyed his field.

Plans for life may not exactly duplicate the process faithfully followed by my father but the similarities are significant. If we expect to accomplish anything in life, we must first select a goal. Distant goals are accomplished by meeting shorter ones that support them. It is extremely rare for one giant step to get us from where we are to where we ultimately want to be. Short- range goals are like short steps. They can take us toward the long- range goal or away from it. When carefully planned and faithfully followed, they move us in the desired direction. When haphazardly selected or carelessly ignored, they will lead us somewhere but not to the ideal goal.

I am appalled when people see little connection between intermediate and distant goals. They profess allegiance to distant goals but act in ways that propel them in an opposite direction. Some declare they want a united family but seldom spend quality time with its members. Some vow they will drink no more alcohol but meet with their drinking buddies every Friday night. Some profess a desire to maintain friendships but make no effort to visit or phone a friend. Most of those people would harshly condemn a hitchhiker who behaved as they. Suppose they saw one standing on a street corner in Dallas, holding a sign that said, "Must get to Miami immediately."

They stop for a traffic light and he yells, "Going to Miami?"
They reply, "No. I'm on my way to L. A."
The hitchhiker yells back, "Mind if I go with you?

We all know that the hitchhiker isn't going to get to Miami very soon if he goes toward L. A. from Dallas. Many of us have done similar things in life and then wonder why we missed our goal. Numerous short-range goals have nothing against them except they add no support to the primary goal. Therefore, they are useless. Any short-range goal that moves us away from the distant goal needs to be altered or it will cause serious delay, if not defeat. Each short-range goal must be measured by something bigger than its self. Short-term goals are crucial because no long-range goal will be reached unless it is under-girded by short-term goals that were systematically and successfully met. They go hand in hand or they don't go.

Movement toward healing and wholeness through "reality therapy" may be illustrated with a fictitious and lengthy parable. Suppose I was unemployed for several months and desperately needed a job. Out of desperation, I borrowed my parents' car to search for employment. A week passed and I had no job and no lead on one.

With my last three dollars in hand, I pulled into a friend's service station and spent two of them for gas. I asked the owner if he needed help. He informed me that business was slow and one helper would be laid off at the end of the week. However, he pointed to a pile of debris beside his business and said he would give it to me if I would remove the usable items and burn the trash.

The thermometer registered one hundred degrees in the shade. I thanked him and declined the offer. Another week passed. I returned to the service station and spent my last dollar for gas. My friend inquired if I had found a job. When he learned I had not, he repeated his former offer.

I took a closer look at the pile of materials and decided it had value. Since I had nothing else to do, I concluded it might be worth my time and effort. The next day, I returned and began to carefully sort the materials.

I first needed to know "What is here?" For days I worked on the project. I found beautiful old timbers of heart pine, something no longer readily available and worth big bucks if you have them. There was a large quantity of old bricks in great demand. Underneath some reusable metal roofing, I found antique windows and doors with many expensive and usable parts. I removed old bent and rusty nails, cut the rotten ends off the boards, stacked each type of material in a separate place and burned the trash.

Having completed that task, I was responsible for the next step. It was my choice to make. Having laboriously discovered "what is" I must decide what I wanted to do with it. As I pondered what to do with what I had, I remembered my parents promised me an acre of land on which to build a house when I wanted it. Building a house eventually became my long-range plan. I alone was responsible for sorting, discarding, moving and reshaping what originally appeared to be little more than a pile of junk.

To my amazement, I gleaned enough material to build a beautiful house. Some of the material needed to be recycled in order to complete the project. I had an excess of some items that I could sell and use the proceeds to purchase items I didn't have. With surprise and delight, I realized what once appeared as a pile of junk could be transformed by me into a much needed and comfortable house. The transformation was accomplished by asking and honestly answering two basic questions, which are: "What is here?" and "What do I want to do with it?" Reality therapy may accomplish a similar transformation in our lives.

At one time or another, all of us have experienced a pile of apparent junk in our lives. Some feel they are a pile of junk. Many of us have sorted through what is there, thrown out the trash, recycled what we could, and moved on. Heavy abusers, addicts and others invariably describe themselves as "no good junk" or with another derogatory term. They have been unable to sort, recycle and rebuild. From where they are, they see junk. From where I am, I see much more. I see in each of them, and each of us, the potential to be a new person.

In order for any of us to become a new person, the two step process mentioned above must occur. We must deliberately discover what is at our disposal and then carefully decide what we want to do with it. Almost without fail, we will be pleasantly surprised by what we find and what we can accomplish. We, like the pile that appeared to be debris, have some remarkable stuff that is there for the taking.

From time to time, each of us may bear some resemblance to a pile of junk. The degree of similarity and frequency may be more prevalent in some than in others. If there is any resemblance, it does not have to remain that way. In the final analysis, we each must choose to be or remain a pile of junk or we can choose to become a new person. We have the ability and responsibility to decide. Our hope for being a new and whole person lies in ascertaining the truth about ourselves and then in carefully deciding what we want to do with it. Transformation and wholeness come by trusting the truth.

Long before this book became a dream, our son composed a poem that succinctly reflects some of the key issues in this chapter.

Fledgling

Let us lift no sad lament
For deeds misdone, time misspent.
Yet drift no more in vain pursuit,
Through stations of the lost, irresolute.
Let spirit soar and soul gracefully glide,
Let passion prevail and truth abide.
With mind outstretched and body bent,
Pursue the quest without relent Overcome
the earth, challenge the sky, Spread your
wings and fly.

William J. Way

CHAPTER 10

Looking for Love

Abuse, addiction, much deviant behavior and perhaps some mental illness are aptly described as "looking for appropriate love in all the wrong places." Everyone has an innate craving and need to love and to be loved. A basic component of human nature atrophies without the proper balance of giving and receiving appropriate love. The primary cause of all abuse, addiction, and deviant behavior may be due to an imbalance of these two. Therefore, we open the door to human health and wholeness by giving and receiving appropriate love.

Due to our nature, everyone is going to love something. Due to our circumstances, some of us will not believe we are loved and some of us will love the wrong thing. We become stunted, maladjusted and sick when we receive too little appropriate love. We experience the same results when we lack the ability or willingness to give or receive proper love. We cannot live without receiving and giving some kind of love.

Everyone is going to love someone or something in some way, with very few exceptions. For our present purposes, "love" is ascribing worth to someone or something. Loving something, ascribing worth to it, is prominently indicated by the behavior of the one who loves. Likewise, behavior also indicates the lack of love for whatever is judged worthless or of little value. Ascribing high value to inappropriate things can be very dangerous and unhealthy. Ascribing low value to important things will also create problems.

Similar results occur when we ascribe worth to too few things or too many things.

There are two basic types of love but it may be called by more than these two names. We describe it best by using opposites. We call it constructive or destructive love, healthy or sick love, and appropriate or inappropriate love. Results are synonymous, regardless of which set of opposites we use.

Throughout life, we respond according to the kind of love received. We need appropriate love modeled for us from birth. Our nature is to love and we are going to ascribe worth to something. We tend to duplicate the kind of love received as a child and practice it as we grow older. If a child was not genuinely loved during its formative years, if it had little or no worth to those responsible for it, the child responded in an unhealthy way.

The child responded differently if it sensed genuine love. An infant does not respond rationally but it has a way of expressing the need for appropriate love and its satisfaction with it. If it was lacking, the child soon demanded some attention, even if from inappropriate love. It is virtually impossible for a person to exist in a vacuum where there is no love because our nature is to love and be loved in some way.

Lack of appropriate love deprives us of a necessary element for human health and wholeness. If appropriate love is not modeled for us, either in infancy or later, the likelihood of our expressing that kind of love is remote and the potential for expressing inappropriate love is extremely high. If there is no one to teach us to love appropriately, there will be someone to teach us to love inappropriately. We may not know the difference and, too often, neither do many of those who teach. Health, wholeness and happiness come only after we experience appropriate love and learn how to return it.

For years, I pondered our urgent necessity to love and be loved. I wondered why a delicate balance is so important to human wholeness. After much pondering, I share some thoughts as an indication of where I am with hope that these may help us give and receive appropriate love. My approach is rooted in the Judeo-Christian tradition but I will refrain from preaching a sermon or asking for a "love offering" at the end of the chapter.

My understanding of human nature is based upon my concept of God. The Bible repeatedly seeks to describe God's nature and his actions. The Old Testament writers speak of God as "The Holy One," "The Loving One," "The One who created out of love," etc. According to them, God bestowed his love on his creation and his love dictated his behavior toward it.

Early Christians also contemplated God's nature and actions. They had access to the ancient Hebrew scriptures that they interpreted in light of Jesus' ministry and the early Christian movement. They eventually summarized God's nature and action with three simple words, found in The New Testament, First John, chapter four, verse sixteen (I John 4:16). It simply says, "God is love." Those words are not as simple as they may first sound. They do not say "God loves" but that he is best described as love. All other attributes of God are encompassed in and interpreted by this one short phrase. God is what he does and does what he is. The two cannot be separated. The nature of God dictates the action of God and both are perfect love.

Ancient people also sought to understand human nature. The Old Testament writers reached an astonishing conclusion on this point. In Genesis, chapter one, verses twenty-six and twenty-seven (Gen. 1: 26-27) they concluded that humanity was "made in God's image" but they did not elaborate. Precisely what they meant by that is hard for us to decipher. Perhaps it means that humanity's distinguishing and basic nature is also love.

If God's nature and action are best described as love and if we are made in his image, then it follows that we are also best described and understood in terms of love. It seems that we, like God, act out of love because that is also our nature. Unlike God, we may love imperfectly and improperly but we will love something in some way. Therefore, to be human is to love something. In order to be a healthy and wholesome person, we must love appropriately.

Our love, whether appropriate or inappropriate, dictates our action. The crucial question isn't where we love or not but rather what do we love and how do we love it? Likewise, our only available choice, when we have one, is what to love and how to love it. Our choices are seriously restricted unless we were fortunate enough to have appropriate love repeatedly modeled for us.

Inquisitive minds ask, "What does it mean to love appropriately?" Ancient biblical writers provide profound insight on this subject. A pithy summary of ancient Israel's religious beliefs is contained in the "Shema," located in Deuteronomy, chapter six, verses four through nine (Deut. 6: 4-9). The "Shema" is a mini catechism and a confession of faith. In it, all are commanded to love God with their heart, soul and mind. Jesus was a devout Jew and the "Shema" was very important for him.

A New Testament passage in Matthew, chapter twenty-two, verses thirty-six through forty (Matt. 22: 36-40), clearly illustrates that fact. Someone requested Jesus identify the greatest commandment. In reply he quotes a portion of the "Shema" and states that the first and greatest commandment is to "Love the Lord your God with all your heart, soul and mind."

Jesus added a second commandment without being asked:

"Love your neighbor as you love yourself."

Jesus continued by saying these two commandments encompass all Judeo-Christian teachings, or "The Law and the Prophets," as he called them. I am particularly interested in Jesus' emphasis upon love. Love is the key ingredient in commandments. He apparently believed humanity's primary purpose and nature are to love appropriately. He further specified what appropriate love requires of humanity.

Appropriate love ascribes the highest worth to God who is valued above all else. It then ascribes equal value to one's self and to one's neighbor, but a value less than for God. Love for everything else is apparently subservient to God, self and neighbor without any priority given. Proper or appropriate love keeps these three in precise position. We can illustrate their proper position and Jesus' teachings by using an equilateral triangle. "God" occupies the apex, above all else. Signifying a position less than "God," "self" and "neighbor" occupy a lower but equal level at the bottom corners.

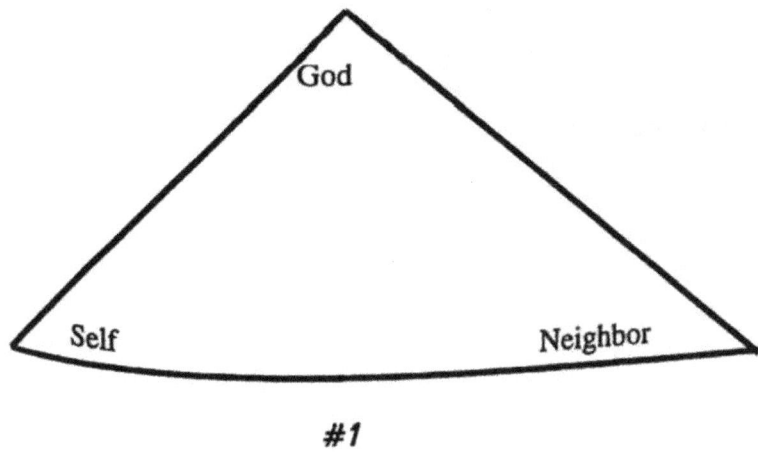

#1

Inappropriate love causes the triangle to tilt and the base to become unbalanced. If "self" is ascribed greater worth than "neighbor," or vice versa, the triangle will tilt so that the one ascribed higher value will be elevated above the ascribed lower value. Anything that causes the triangle to tilt in any direction is inappropriate love.

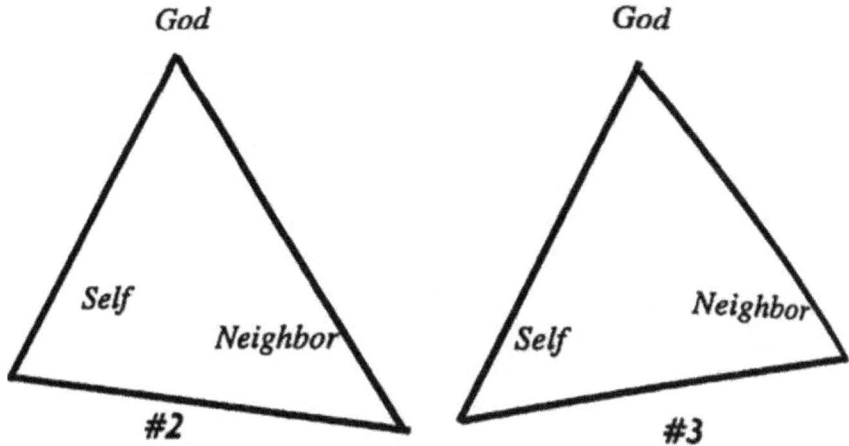

Anything that destroys the triangle, either by omitting one of the three or by replacing one of them, is also inappropriate love. If we consider ourselves more important than anything else, including God, we destroy the triangle by removing one point or by usurping God's position. If we elevate our neighbor or anything other than

God to the highest value, we make appropriate love impossible and destroy the triangle by deleting God and by usurping God's place. In Judeo-Christian terms, that is idolatry. It can also be easily illustrated with our triangle.

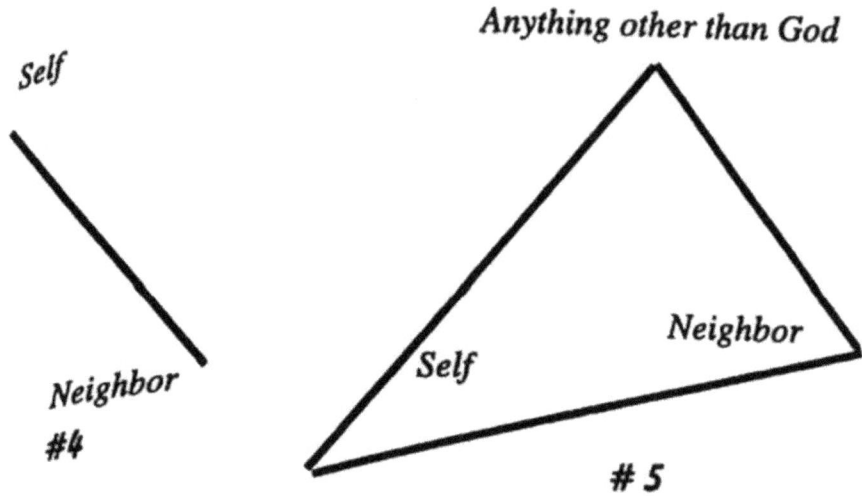

These two commandments given by Jesus not only encompass all Judeo-Christian teachings, but also encompass the human condition. The commandment for us to love "God" above all else is not just a religious commandment. It is also a statement of fact. Our "god" is whatever we love most, whatever we ascribe the highest worth. The basic principle remains the same, whether used in a religious or secular sense. If it controls us, it is therefore our "god," be it the Judeo-Christian God or something else. The case of the first letter separates the two, i.e., "God" or "god" respectively, and reflects radical differences in human belief and behavior.

Ancient Hebrew writers and Jesus were absolutely correct. Whatever we love most is our "god" and it gets priority in our heart, soul and mind. Given that fact, it is only a matter of time before we appropriate the image of the ultimate in our life and reflect its image in our behavior.

The devotee of a divine assumes characteristics of divine behavior. "Workaholics" work. "Playboys" play. Egotistical and selfish people demonstrate excessive concern for themselves. "Overeaters" display excessive weight that reflects their highest value. An abuser of alcohol frequently smells like alcohol, thinks about alcohol and seeks alcohol. In almost every area of our life, the image appropriation process provides a clear clue to what we value most, our "god."

The second commandment of Jesus precisely and concisely states the human condition. "Love your neighbor as you love yourself," said Jesus. Appropriate love always ascribes equal value for neighbor and for self. One is just as important as the other. A subtle twist in this simple sounding statement indicates the ingenious mind of Jesus. We have no problem accepting his statement as a religious directive for the proper treatment of our neighbor but it is much more than that. There is another profound, disturbing and often unseen truth contained in what he said.

According to Jesus, we always love our neighbor as we love ourselves! There is no exception. It is impossible to love self in one way and love our neighbor differently. If we love one appropriately, we must also love the other appropriately. Conversely, if we love one inappropriately then we also love the other inappropriately. The base of the previously mentioned triangle is simultaneously balanced or unbalanced for both. They cannot be separated. The value placed on each may not be equal but the kind of love is always the same, always either appropriate or inappropriate for both.

The two great commandments given by Jesus include more than first imagined. The primary point of each is love, or ascribing worth to something or someone. Each is an invitation and an admonition to a particular lifestyle and behavior pattern. They encompass the essence of Judeo-Christian faith and prescribe behavior conducive to health and wholeness.

Therefore, adherence to the Judeo-Christian religion is not measured by verbally accepting the validity of these principles but by reflecting appropriate love in our behavior. Furthermore, anyone acting primarily from inappropriate love has rejected the Judeo- Christian lifestyle, even though they may verbally and vehemently profess allegiance to it.

Many people believe these two commandments contain nothing more than religious invitations and admonitions. Others are surprised and delighted to learn they reflect fundamental and factual statements that succinctly describe the principles by which everyone lives. These fundamental principles are applicable in a religious or secular sense and offer meaning to human life.

Most of us have some understanding of their religious application. A secular application may require more thought. Since "god" is what we value most and directs our life, an addict's "god" is that to which he/she is addicted. Heavy abusers have a particular "god" that controls them. Therefore, appropriate love is impossible because the mandatory and balanced triangle cannot be maintained. Addiction and abuse destroy the triangle by usurping God's place. Conversely, appropriate love of self eliminates the abuse of drugs, alcohol, food, etc. Appropriate love of our neighbor eliminates murder, sexual abuse, racism, stealing, slander, etc. These principles encompass every aspect of life, both in a religious or secular sense.

All of life is now interrupted in terms of love, or ascribing worth. Our nature is love and our actions reflect what and how we love. In light of this, religion and life are described in terms of what and how we love.

Using religious terms, "sin" is inappropriate love, loving the wrong thing, or sick love. "Salvation" is appropriate love, healthy love, or having the prescribed triangle balanced. "Atonement" is "at-one-ment," being at one with God and imitating his love in action as best we can.

Secular language can also describe life in terms of love. Destructive human behavior results from and is an expression of inappropriate or sick love. Well-adjusted personalities and wholesome, genuinely happy people are those who love appropriately. A purposeful and meaningful life comes primarily to those who love appropriately by treating others and themselves with respect. Additional comments may enhance our understanding of what it means to properly love ourselves as we love our neighbor. The complex connotations of "love" make it most difficult to define.

Were it as simple as a kiss, it would be much easier to understand. A kiss, I am told, is mouthful of nothing that tastes like heaven and sounds like an old cow pulling her foot out of mud! Love is definitely more complex. Any words used to describe love are always insufficient and incomplete.

Love is bigger than ourunderstanding of it. "God is love," and we cannot fully understand God. If we could, that would make us greater than God. In spite of our inadequacies, we have been entrusted with partial truth that must guide us for now. I formulated the following statement to clarify my comprehension of appropriate love for self and neighbor.

"It is wanting for everyone, others and myself, what is best for us and wanting it to the degree I am willing to make some effort and sacrifice in order for us to have it."

From the Judeo-Christian perspective, that is precisely how God acts toward us. We are made in his image and fulfill both our nature and purpose only when we act like him. That kind of love ascribes worth through action. It is the proper kind of love for a friend or an enemy. It is creative, whereas all other love is destructive.

It is difficult to always love appropriately, especially if we don't know how or what it is. A young Air Force officer in pilot training boldly declared love for his wife during a class I taught. He then added, "And just to prove it, I beat the hell out of her every day."

Class members gave him a big laugh.

Without even a smile, I replied, "I don't know what you love but I am sure you do not love your wife appropriately. Genuinely loving someone and beating the hell out of them are absolutely impossible." The young officer got mad, stood up and acted as if he wanted to demonstrate his "love" for me. I had no fear. I knew who would suffer most if he dared express his kind of love toward me. He was a Lieutenant and I was a Lieutenant Colonel.

Healthy and wholesome love for others is demonstrated by a willingness to help them and to sacrifice something for their good. "Beating the hell out of them," is definitely not that kind of love. Likewise, figuratively or literally beating up on myself is not healthy love.

A lady in a taxi on a cold and rainy day demonstrated appropriate love. She spotted a thin, elderly and ill clad lady waiting for a bus. Her discomfort was extremely obvious. The passenger in the taxi instructed the driver to stop.

The passenger invited the elderly lady, a stranger, into the cab and informed her the ride would be free. The original passenger instructed the cab driver to take the elderly lady wherever she needed to go. After the two ladies were safely delivered to their destinations and the first had paid the bill, the taxi driver related the event to a friend and said, "I guess that is what you call genuine love." He was correct!

Since our nature is to love something in some way, what is the origin of appropriate and healthy love in us? The opening paragraphs of this chapter offered some hints. It certainly does not appear to be automatic or all would exhibit it in our actions. We human beings have the necessity and potential to love but without certain outside contributions it seems almost impossible for a person to love appropriately. Inappropriate love apparently comes from the outside too. Since we are communal creatures, we always receive one or the other. Given our nature, apparently, we can get both only from another. Someone who has it must give it to us. Our knowledge of human growth and development provides strong clues to the origin of love in us.

Appropriate and inappropriate love probably comes by osmosis, being subconsciously absorbed from those who possess it and share it. Children experience being loved and later learn how to talk about it. Love is birthed and nurtured in experience, not reason. Infancy and early childhood are critical for a child's experience of love, regardless of its type. Children absorb whatever is around them.

We know young children mimic parents in their walk, talk, mannerisms, etc. It seems only natural that they would also imitate the way they love, whether healthy or sick. A child's experiences of

love are embedded in its brain, or somewhere, and the child later reproduces the kind of love experienced in its formative years. Therefore, dysfunctional parents and families lack healthy love and their child has little knowledge or experience of it.

Families that practice appropriate love tend to produce emotionally healthy children, often without a conscious effort to do so. The truth may be that many families periodically practice both appropriate and inappropriate love. Total perfection and complete degradation are almost impossible to find in any family or person. However, one type likely dominates.

My older brother evidenced learning ability and the mimicking process of a very small child. He was playing with his box of meager and simple toys when something caused them to spill. He said an ugly word. Our mother did not clearly understand him and asked, "What did you say?" He said it again. Our mother sternly reprimanded him for saying such a word and concluded with, "We don't talk like that in this family." He looked up at her and innocently replied, "Papa do when he spills the taters." His words illustrated a child's appropriation of language and perhaps its appropriation of love.

Can a person who received no healthy love ever be able to love appropriately? Due to our nature and developmental process, it may be remotely possible but highly unlikely. I heard that a blind hog finds a few acorns, so these people could possibly stumble upon something, at least in theory. Given the reproductive quality of love, persons in this category are primarily committed to the type of love shown them and share the same type of love with their children. The vicious circle continues ever outward until they experience wholesome love from another.

Let us ask a slightly different question. If childhood experiences primarily determine how one initially loves, can a person move from inappropriate or sick love to appropriate or healthy love? They can move, but only with outside help. Therefore, they are not automatically and forever doomed to exist in sick love. They may be sick but there is a chance to get healthy if someone offers them enough healthy love. They may be transformed by experiencing healthy love from anyone capable of giving it. Their transformation may come at any point between childhood and death. However, the catalyst for transformation is identical to that which initially enables a child to participate in healthy love, i.e., receiving healthy love from another or by being infused with healthy love from the outside. Appropriate love always comes from being in the presence of like love, initially or as a healing process. The ramification and application of this truth boggle the mind.

Being in the presence of appropriate love may be recognized differently by an infant than by an adult. An infant first experiences it, without knowing what it is. If it is present, the infant senses it. It is experienced before it is understood or verbalized.

Anyone beyond early childhood may also discover the meaning of appropriate love by the same process. However, I suspect those who are later transformed from sick to healthy love get there in the reverse order. They are prone to first conceptualize it, then verbalize it and eventually recognize it has come to them. For those beyond early childhood, the transformation process produces a conflict between the old love and the new. When someone initially offers them appropriate love, they are often reluctant to accept it because they suspect it is the sick type. An infant accepts it without hesitation.

Such love is difficult to recognize when offered by a stranger to one who does not know what it is. Repeated receptions of proper love by someone beyond childhood elicit thought, analysis and verbalization. When they recognize that appropriate love has been received, they respond, "I am genuinely loved." Receiving and recognizing healthy love enables one to respond in kind, whether initially as a child or following a transformation.

If healthy love comes to us by receiving it from others, whether initially or moving from sick to healthy love, we now have a major directive for wholesome and helpful human behavior. Our intended nature and purpose are to participate in appropriate love. Reflecting and sharing appropriate love are our directives for family life, for participating in Judeo-Christian religion, for administering all rehabilitation efforts and for a wholesome everyday life, to specifically mention only a few. This directive provides the purpose for being and the process by which to function.

A common cry heard today is, "What can the family do to favorably influence their children and help them avoid devastating choices?" The answer may be less sophisticated than expected but answers that sound simple may be difficult to accomplish. Since children largely duplicate the type of love expressed in the family, healthy families are necessary for children to receive and practice healthy love.

The most important gift parents can give to their children is appropriate love, not status or material possessions. The latter two are important, but not most important. Children who know they are genuinely loved are empowered to overcome numerous obstacles

And thrive even when material things are in short supply. Children need and want appropriate love more than anything else. Adult family members desperately need it and can never find complete fulfillment without it. This is our nature. Given that fact, expressing appropriate love is the top priority for any family.

Every family, and every family member, is less than perfect, regardless of what a husband or wife may say about their first mate or the person they almost married. Every family must struggle to maintain a proper balance of giving and receiving appropriate love. Mistakes will be made but genuine love provides a corrective process and allows for those mistakes to be made and corrected. There are no guarantees that certain behavior will produce desired results. Genuine love allows for trial and error, democratic decisions, open discussion, different opinions, etc.

For unknown reasons, some family members may not feel genuinely loved at all times and in all situations. If such adverse situations can be resolved, they will only be resolved through appropriate love. It, and only it, gives freedom. With the rewards so great and the alternative so devastating, everything else must take a secondary position to appropriate love in the family.

Appropriate love builds families, relationships, self-esteem, reserved strengths, resistance to enticing pitfalls, etc. Appropriate family love has the miraculous power to transform the world because every person is born into a family. When genuine love is absent, family members tend to see themselves as worthless and no good, regardless of status and possessions. Having reached that conclusion, they begin a downward spiral by loving the wrong thing and by searching for appropriate love in inappropriate places. That devastating journey continues until they destroy themselves or until someone demonstrates appropriate love and they recognize what it is and live by it.

The above mentioned "devastating journey" can be easily seen in the lives of ordinary people and families. I have performed the wedding ceremony for numerous couples. I counseled many more whose marriages were in serious trouble. Almost without fail, marital trouble is rooted in inappropriate love, much of which was first practiced in the birth family. Time and time again, they married for the wrong reason.

They were in love but loved the wrong thing. Some married because all their friends were getting married. Some sought prestige, security or freedom from nagging parents. There were those who wanted to escape loneliness and singleness. A number of them wanted someone to keep house, shop, wash, iron, or earn a paycheck. Some married in order to legalize their sexual activity or relieve a guilty conscience.

When any one of these is the primary reason for marriage, known or unknown, the chance for a happy and meaningful marriage is greatly diminished, if not destroyed. There should be no surprise when these marriages falter or fail. Failed marriages frequently affect people and they then tend to seek solace in less than appropriate ways, including drugs, alcohol, illicit sex and instant remarriage. They look for love in all the wrong places. Momentary relief may come but the pain soon returns in ever increasing quantity. Without outside assistance, they have little hope for healing and wholeness, in marriage or life.

Many failed marriages legally survived long enough to produce children. Some couples entered into a legal marriage only because a child had already been conceived. Having been birthed in a bruised relationship and having been surrounded by inappropriate love, these children are prime candidates for severe problems throughout life. Without outside intervention, they will most likely enter the painful and futile search for appropriate love in all the wrong places.

We need no longer ask, "What can the family do to salvage our children and our world?" The hard task is doing what we know ought to be done for every one's benefit. The family's primary purpose is practicing appropriate love. Our greatest hope for healthy families begins and ends with that kind of love.

Given the fact that appropriate love is infused by those who possess and are possessed by it, we have a powerful directive and corrective for participation in the Judeo-Christian faith. The essence of Judeo-Christian religion encompasses appropriate love for God, others and self. That is the core from which everything else evolves. Sacrificial and unselfish giving for the good of God, others and self is the central theme from creation to Christendom. That is the nature of the creator and the created.

True followers of the faith practice and participate in that kind of love at home, work and worship. They participate in a singular lifestyle wherever they are. Religious behavior is not reserved for Sunday worship, for when the pastor is present or not for special effect. Even though followers of the faith have freely received undeserved love, they dare not take the gift lightly. They refuse to believe it can be easily bought, bartered or earned. They do not gleefully sow their wild oats on Saturday night and nonchalantly attend a worship service on Sunday to pray for a crop failure, even though full forgiveness is readily available.

True adherents are the first to recognize that perfect love is humanly impossible. It is the goal toward which we move, having freely received perfect love from our creator. As true adherents, we seek to appropriate the image of God in our life and to reflect that image in all we do and are.

Without wanting to be judgmental, there are individuals and groups who apparently draw other conclusions. Under the disguise of being a part of the Judeo-Christian community, they emphasize a "what's in it for me" approach. In their religion, the role of God and neighbor is to help them get what they want without serious concern for what God and others need or want.

Other professing adherents prescribe a mathematical formula for human live that guarantees complete heavenly bliss even while on earth. Concern for the next life consumes some people and they forget to make the present one all it can be for themselves and others. If Judeo-Christian religion, or any religion, has lost some of its appeal and is in decline, there may be a legitimate reason. It, like marriages and individuals, cannot and will not survive unless it operates from appropriate love. All organizations, groups and individuals who profess Judeo- Christian faith must faithfully practice appropriate love or else they cease to be what they profess.

Rehabilitation centers and programs, as well as individual efforts, are truly successful only when they convince patients they are lovable, loved (have worth), and are capable of learning to respond with appropriate love. Rehabilitation and recovery do not begin in the mind but in one's experience. Appropriate love must first be demonstrated by the staff, or someone, and then experienced by the patient. Staff members and helpers who do not embody appropriate love will be unable to jump-start or support patients and will be detrimental to the healing process.

Any program or person with a primary motive other than appropriate love for the patient is detrimental to the transformation process. All patients in rehabilitation may not be brilliant but they are usually smart enough to detect if they have worth to those who administer the program. They cannot be fooled for long because many patients have more intellectual acumen than some helpers, particularly about abuse and addiction. We should not be surprised at the low transformation rate and the high rate of recidivism when we note the circumstances under which many rehabilitation efforts began and the procedures by which workers were recruited. As an addendum, comments about treatment centers and professional treatment programs apply to individual helpers, family members, well-meaning friends and private counselors.

I repeatedly recommended the "appropriate love approach" to administrators and other staff members in programs where I worked but with little favorable results. Program restraints, my position as a chaplain without a medical or specialized degree to validate my approach, their desire for job security, etc., prevented responsible persons from pursuing my recommendations.

I kept trying because almost every patient with whom I used this approach responded very favorably and frequently gave me accolades. This recommended formula for transformation is no accident. It has been successfully used before. Judeo-Christian religion emphasizes the sacrificial and loving efforts of God who demonstrates love for and worth of his creation. God also elicits similar love from his creation so that each and every person may find a meaningful life.

My proposed approach to recovery, either in a treatment center or elsewhere, is primarily a human duplication of that divine approach. That kind of love fosters rehabilitation of any type, whether offered by an individual or group. This approach was not initially designed to be a "religious" approach. My open-minded search eventually led me to my present position.

I experimented with many things but this is the only thing that made sense to me. Likewise, my approach was the only thing patients and clients willingly accepted. I patiently followed their leads and mine to this point. I presented and practiced it without apology or religious jargon.

This approach is "religious" without a religious name. Its two directives are to love appropriately and act accordingly. It elicits like love but it does not coerce or condemn. It grants freedom for a person to stay where they are but it encourages them to move to something less painful.

It equalizes the playing field for the participants because no one is superior to the other. It is designed to meet the needs of someone who hurts and not some selfish need of the one who seeks to be religious or receive their own reward. It is religion in action instead of words. Even though we are only human, we are capable of imitating divine love and do not have to be "preachy" about our practice of it.

Committed to that love, recognized and declared religious or otherwise, we are empowered and encouraged to love others and ourselves appropriately. Motivated and empowered by that love, we want for others and ourselves what is best, to the degree we will sacrifice for it. By whatever name we call this approach, the principle remains the same for all healthy rehabilitation. Appropriate love, offered from others and accepted by one who needs it, is the prescription for renewal.

Specific comments are in order for anyone who has entertained the idea that they need a transformation from sick to healthy love. If you desire to practice appropriate love, you can seek it, even if no one has recently offered it to you. There comes a point at which we each must assume responsibility for ourselves because there is a limit to what one person can do for another. It is time you dare to believe you have great worth.

If you have religious leanings, accept that fact because God does not create junk and he loves his creation. If you are not religious, accept that you are important because you are a unique human being with great potential. Accept it on the basis of total available evidence and not on the basis of some sick person's words and actions.

Consider who it was that convinced you that you were worthless. I do not know precisely who it was but I strongly suspect it was someone who also thought they were worthless. That is the way it works. Sick people can make other people sick! It is legitimate to question and disagree with the repeated pronouncements and judgments of any uniformed and sick parent or person. You may have drawn your authority to act from an invalid source. Verify the source responsible for that negative judgment and compare it with other available evidence.

Improper and defective sources give us authority to act and may unknowingly be affirmed as helpful. There is an urgency to consciously question the validity and truth of every source. Known and valid sources enable us to make a firm stand.

At one of my military assignments, regulations required each technical school student spend four hours in a special class facilitated by a chaplain. As the senior chaplain in that division, I was responsible for scheduling chaplain coverage for each class. Without warning, I received a phone call from a low-ranking airman who informed me I had only two hours allotted for each class.

I asked, "On whose authority?"

He forcefully replied, "On my authority, sir."

Regardless of what I said to him, he would not change his decision. I politely asked for his name, rank and phone number. I further informed him that as soon as our conversation ended I was going to call the Wing Commander and inform him that airman so-and-so, at his phone number, had just assumed the authority to supersede an Air Force regulation. I would further ask the Commander what I should do, follow the Air Force regulation or obey the airman?

He said, "Would you repeat that, sir?"

I slowly repeated what I had just told him.

After a long pause he asked, "Sir, will you delay that call until I call you right back?"

I assured him I would wait for his return call. In just a few minutes, I received another phone call.

"Sir, this is Airman so-and-so. Do you remember me?"

I assured him I did.

He continued, "Do you remember what we talked about?"

I assured him I remembered.

He replied, "Well Sir, will you just forget I called? You still have four hours for each class."

A valid source gives us authority to act. We do well to know the source authorizing every action. Our ultimate source is inevitably connected to our "god." Healthy and wholesome acts stem from competent and constructive sources. Unknown and destructive sources also empower us. It is extremely important to know what is valid, competent and constructive. I knew what that Air Force regulation required and I acted accordingly without doubt or hesitation.

During difficult times, we tend to forget our authority and need a reminder, if we have ever known. With information drawn from a reliable source, life may not be as problematic as we originally thought.

A young lady was very fond of a country boy who courted her. On a very cool evening, they sat in the porch swing, she at one end and he at the other. Desiring a closer association, she initiated a conversation designed to move him closer to her.

Drawing from an invalid source, she pitifully proclaimed, "No one loves me and my hands are so cold."

The lad was equal to the occasion and authoritatively replied, "God loves you and you can sit on your hands.

It is wise to always remember that somebody really loves you and you have the authority to change your situation for the better. That comes from a valid source!

If it is difficult to believe that others appropriately love you, practice appropriate love for yourself. That is the other half of appropriate human love. You may have little control over the treatment you receive from others but you can assume major control over the way you treat yourself. Recall our definition of love includes working to get what is best for you. Most of us can easily identify areas where improvement would make our life less painful and more productive. Most of us are aware of things that hurt others and us.

Minor changes in our verbal response to others, in what we put into our bodies, in where we spend our time, etc., will produce major changes if we continue such practices. Others are more likely to favorably respond to us when demonstrate appropriate love for them and ourselves. However, a few people are going to appropriately love us, no matter what, but they are extremely scarce.

We can possibly increase that number by properly loving ourselves and by demonstrating that love in our action.

If you are not receiving appropriate love where you are, move to a place where such love is much more likely to be found. A change in scenery or behavior may work wonders. If appropriate love is lacking where you work or live, it may be wise to relocate to a well-chosen place. If your "friends" are not offering appropriate love, find new friends in new places where such love is more likely to be.

If you are involved in an unhappy marriage or a troublesome family life, initiate action designed to restore wholeness. Change your behavior and do something different that is designed to help.

Marriages are often improved by seeking a competent and professional counselor. The advice of well-meaning friends and acquaintances can create more problems than it solves.

A young lady visited my office and asked that I perform a wedding ceremony for her and her boyfriend. I advised her I would agree to conduct a wedding only after I had talked with the couple. She quickly informed me that she needed no counseling. I inquired why she felt that way. She told me she had talked at great length about marriage with her girlfriend.

When asked what qualified her friend as a marriage counselor, she said, "She knows all there is to know about marriage. She's been married five times!"

We must be careful to whom we listen when we seek a place where appropriate love is more likely to be found. With some caution and effort, such a place can be located.

Persons longing for proper love are encouraged to join groups that practice appropriate love. If you are drinking more and enjoying it less, you are a prime candidate for A.A. I know of no other group more motivated by sacrificial love. Faithful members of that group will pay almost any price and bear any burden for another who wants to get and remain sober. No other group is more accepting and forgiving or asks fewer questions.

There is a similar group, N.A., for anyone with a drug problem. Numerous other specific groups exist for the sole purpose of helping people change their behavior as they learn to properly care for themselves and others. Synagogues and churches that fulfill their purpose are ideal groups to join because they practice appropriate love. Moreover, they offer courses and training sessions for those who wish to participate. Anyone who is looking for appropriate love need not search alone, but a bit of caution is advised.

If appropriate love for others is not prominent in your life, practice what you already know about it. Most of us know enough to get started. We know what is decent and kind or what others have done to delight us. We can risk doing something for someone just because we believe it will help and because we want to help, with no strings attached. Play "Boy Scout" and help some old lady cross the street, if she needs help. Cut the grass for a sick neighbor before they hire it done. Find someone who apparently wonders if they have value to anyone and prove they are valuable to you. All the above, and more, can be easily, economically, and safely done. The real value is that such activities may spark a flame that can never be extinguished. Use your present ability to love others appropriately and it will most likely increase.

All of us are looking for love. That is our nature. We will love something in some way. Inappropriate love enables us to exist temporarily. Appropriate and healthy love changes mere existence into meaningful and joyful living. Inappropriate love tends to diminish any good qualities we have in us. Appropriate love is creative and constructive, enabling the good in us to grow.

When we fail to love what is beneficial for us, we love what is detrimental to us. Regardless of where we are at this moment, it behooves us to seriously consider how we may enhance appropriate love. We can begin where we are. Caring for a pet is cheaper and less addictive than vodka. A honeymoon with the right mate is more fun than sessions with a psychiatrist. Appropriately loving and leading an offspring is the most important and enjoyable job in the world. Appropriate love for God, neighbor and self is the only thing that provides human health, wholeness and happiness. May that be our constant guide while looking for love, both to give and to receive.

CHAPTER 11

Driven by a Dream

There is a provocative story that I have embellished and whose authenticity is irrelevant. The administrative personnel of college decided to select its most outstanding student. The debated how that should be done. Some suggested the professors select the person by a vote. After deliberation, they concluded that would only identify the student known by the most professors. Someone proposed that the student body vote on the matter. That proposal was also discarded because it would identify the most popular student on campus, not the most outstanding. Eventually, someone suggested the new computer could easily accomplish the task because it could be programmed to make a fair and unbiased selection. All agreed to have the computer make the choice.

Plans for the event were publicized and invitations were sent to parents, alumni, students and interested people. On the designated day, a huge crowd gathered in the college auditorium. The president's private secretary sat by the computer that was loaded with data cards and directives. He gave her a signal. She flipped a switch and the computer went to work. It hummed, buzzed, clicked and clacked for a little while and then stopped. A single card fell into a slot. The secretary gave it to a runner who rushed it to the waiting president and audience.

Anxiously, he silently read the name on the card and turned red. He called his advisors together for a quick conference and informed them he could not announce the name. The student whose name appeared on the card was known by many to be exactly opposite of what they expected. He had long, dirty hair. If he owned a comb, he did not use it.

From his body odor, apparently, he thought deodorant was the name of a Rock group in California and he had no intentions of associating with it. He often wore plaid pants and a striped shirt with sandals and no socks. His clothes were usually wrinkled and soiled. None of the other students spent more time in his presence than was absolutely necessary. No one agreed to be his roommate.

He was disliked so much that even his imaginary friends refused to associate with him! His scholastic ability was in question. He had failed several courses and his final grades for the previous semester included a "C-" in two subjects, a "D" in two, and an "F" in another. He enrolled for the present semester only because the president granted special dispensation. The president knew all that information and therefore would not announce the name.

The president's advisors argued that he could not refuse to accept the name because the computer selected it. To deny the choice of the computer would jeopardize its future use for major decisions. The president agreed with them, slowly walked to the podium and reluctantly read the name. Upon hearing the selected name, the students responded with raucous laughter.

The president assured them it was no joke and asked the named student to come forward. He was not present. Several people were dispatched to find him and bring him to the gathering. Someone found him walking barefoot in the goldfish pond. When informed of his selection, he also laughed. Eventually, they persuaded him to accompany them to the auditorium.

Down the aisle he came. Every eye in the building was focused on him. He was a sight to behold! He had a head full of unkempt hair. As was often the case, he was wearing dirty plaid slacks, now with one wet leg, along with that wrinkled stripped shirt. On his dirty feet he wore wet floppy sandals and no socks. Those by whom he passed also knew he wore no deodorant. He sheepishly made his way to the podium as the audience sat in stunned silence. The president presented him to the audience and immediately adjourned the meeting.

Those attending went away thinking the day and project had been a complete failure. However, it was not! Something happened to the lad whose name was announced as the most outstanding student. Within a few days, he found his comb and frequently used it on his clean, fresh-cut hair. Within a few weeks, other students noticed him wearing color coordinated clothes, including socks. When he came near, it was obvious he was using deodorant and cologne.

He was friendly with other students and began to hang out with them. Professors noticed improvements in class attendance, participation and grades. Improvements continued throughout that semester and all remaining semesters. At graduation, he was on the Dean's list, voted "most congenial" and "most likely to succeed." The change occurred because he was driven by a dream.

The rest of the story illustrates the compelling power of a dream. Years later, the president's secretary told what actually happened. After the spectacular announcement, she returned to collect the data cards and restore them to their proper place. To her amazement, she discovered the computer had malfunctioned and stopped without completing its assigned task. The card fell into the slot by accident, not by the computer's choice. Not knowing what to do, she did nothing and kept the secret for years.

The above story emphasizes a statement attributed to Carl Sandburg who reportedly said, "Nothing happens unless first a dream." There is more than one kind of dream. There are dreams that come while we are asleep and there are dreams that come while we are very much awake. Even though the former type is profoundly interesting and important, our primary attention is devoted to the latter.

Dreams that come while we are awake are also known as aspirations, longings, expectations, deep desires, visions, etc. Many of them are usually considered desirable, possible or probable. Without giving it much thought, we have normally assumed such dreams are always positive. However, my association with persons suffering from a severe pain in their gut taught me that apparently most of their dreams are not positive by any stretch of the imagination. Having discovered that, I began to better understand their thinking and behavior. If dreams reflect or harbor expectations and what we often consider possible or probable, people with low self-esteem must have negative dreams. Those who firmly believe they are "no good" primarily expect pain and failure in their life and will work hard to make that become a reality. Without realizing it, they too are driven by a dream, but it is negative. Even though their dream may be negative, it empowers them for action. If this is true, we have another remarkable revelation into human behavior.

For what do we dream? The presence or absence of a positive or negative dream tells much about a person. Those with a positive dream are empowered to press onward and upward. Those with a negative dream tend to suffer, wither and die.

Many abusers of alcohol reported they did not dream while asleep. I have some skepticism about their report because alcohol affects the brain and they may be unable to remember when they dream. When confronted with my doubts about their report, many of them adamantly affirmed it. I am convinced the phenomenon deserves further consideration.

After pondering their report, I immediately wondered if they dreamed while they were awake. I questioned them. They, and I, originally thought in terms of positive dreams. The question was asked numerous times and in many different groups but seldom did anyone give evidence of having a positive dream.

Eventually, I made the connection. They do dream while awake but the dreams are almost exclusively negative until and unless someone helps them adjust. The secret to their unhealthy and unwise behavior was uncovered by the revelation that they too were empowered by a dream, a negative dream. Seen from that perspective, their irrational inexplicable behavior became somewhat rational. Having made that discovery about those who abuse alcohol, I also suspect it is true for those who abuse anything or lack self-esteem.

The presence and power of negative dreams provide a prominent clue for understanding behavior and for facilitating recovery. People who have only negative dreams give up all expectations for life to get better. They have experienced more than their share of life's misery. If they previously had positive dreams, they were painfully shattered too many times to risk any more. They are afraid to risk, reach or resume hope. Their battery has lost its starting power.

Their fuel tank is empty. The magnetism of the future has no pull on them. They believe they are stuck, that their future is dark, and that life will only be more painful. Their only hope, as they see it, is temporary relief through use of alcohol, drugs, or whatever they abuse. Their downward spiral can be interrupted only with a powerful positive dream that will likely be sparked by another person.

Abusers of drugs and alcohol are not the only people who have ceased to dream positively. As indicated above, all types of abusers fit this description. Young and old, as well as rich and poor, have negative dreams. Persons in prolonged poverty, victims of unending oppression, persons who suffer from an incurable disease and numerous others tend to have no positive dreams. Recovery from addiction, adversity and lethargy is primarily predicated on being empowered by a positive dream.

Since people are driven by their dreams, we can identify a prominent impetus for harmful behavior and a possible corrective for many of those who presently suffer. Those who facilitate recovery for abusers and those who minister to the unfortunate have one primary task. That task is to encourage, enlighten and enable others to find a positive and realistic dream that empowers them. On one hand, the task is so simple it eludes us but, on the other hand, it is so difficult it is almost impossible. A few years ago, Dr. Martin Luther King, Jr. demonstrated how a positive dream empowered people and radically changes the status quo.

Dreams deserve careful consideration and evaluation. Each of us would do well to carefully consider our dreams. We should discern if they are positive, negative or nonexistent. Dreams apparently propel us toward the future. An astute awareness of our dreams provides helpful insight into the direction of our travel. If we have no positive dream, or if they are weak it is advisable to develop them. If our present condition negates positive dreams, it is time to seek professional help or prepare for mishaps. If we have hung on to an unfulfilled dream, it may be time to reevaluate it, with a competent counselor, in order to refurbish or release it. The lack of positive dream, or if they are weak it is advisable to develop them, dream is one problem but giving up too quickly on a long held positive dream is another. We may be much closer to realizing it than we thought. Minor adjustments in thought or behavior may enable us to fulfill the dream.

A man shared with me his powerful and unfulfilled dream. He felt he had been called to be a minister. He dropped out of school long before completing the twelfth grade. He was the father of four or five young children. His meager income came from a small farm and hauling pulpwood. Our church requires advanced education for ordination but he had no opportunity or financial means to acquire it.

From his perspective, there was no way to fulfill his dream. He was devastated. After a lengthy conversation, I ask what "ministry" meant to him. "Helping others," be responded.

I asked if he thought professional education was necessary in order for a person to help another or was it possible to help others with what you have and where you are. After pondering and discussing that for a while, be smiled and exclaimed, "That's it. I can do ministry where I am and with what I have."

That adjustment to his dream made him a new man. He was deeply disturbed when he came to see me but exuberant when he departed. In the days and weeks that followed, be became a leading layman in his church. If it was cold, he went early to turn on the heat. If it was hot, he went early to turn on the air conditioner. If something needed special attention at the church, he took care of it. If the neighbors were ill or injured, he looked after them.

He was driven by a dream and he was ministering with what he had. The fulfillment of his dream was closer than realized. A little professional help enable him to grasp it. Similar results are possible for many who hold positive and unfulfilled dreams.

Many people seeking recovery are very close to radical transformation by way of a positive dream. Left to their own insights and strengths, they will never discover it. Even though they are so close to it they, for numerous reasons, do not see it or will not dare admit it is there.

A keen counselor or an astute friend can often spot it lurking just around the corner. The helper enables them to see, find and express the dream. Even though this is easier to say than do, it is surprising how effective a competent helper can be in enabling a positive dream to be born or reborn in another.

Regardless of their present condition or their history, almost every person seriously seeking recovery will express a positive dream to someone who has treated them with dignity and respect. The birth of a positive dream is a sure sign that recovery has begun.

Over time and under favorable conditions, most people can be encouraged and enticed to dream again for a better life. There is an innate hunger for health and wholeness that surfaces when it is safe to dream positively.

It is urgent for us to dream but our dreams should be checked against reality. We are wise when we tether dreams to truth. Negative and positive dreams often require alteration when subjected to the truth. Some will be destroyed but others will be rejuvenated.

A positive and possible dream developed during one's energetic youth or early adult life may require alteration when confronted by age and infirmity. There may have been nothing wrong with the dream but one's ability to fulfill it can diminish. When that is the case, it is time to admit the truth and revamp our dream.

I once dreamed of being a great football player. For my size, I was very fast and extremely strong. Long after I was an adult, my nickname was "The Wheel" because people said my feet moved so fast when I ran that they looked like wheels. I never became a great football player because I never played football. My parents did not allow me to play high school football because they were afraid, I would hurt somebody! I surrendered that dream. Mother Nature, Father Time, astuteness and arthritis have combined to convince me that dream is impractical. I now have other dreams that drive me.

One new dream is to write a book. Reality reminds me of the necessity to address issues about which I have knowledge and fresh insights. Many years of experience and study in the field of alcohol and drug rehabilitation provided a framework from which I can write and about which I now dream of sharing something valuable.

If freedom is possible, truth is the only thing that will set us free from our negative dreams. The significance of this point cannot be over emphasized. Negative dreams are most frequently based on erroneous information and assumptions that can be shattered by confrontation with the truth.

Someone who, from early childhood, believed they were worthless also dreamed for life to get progressively worse and it usually did. If that person experienced appropriate love and discovered a different source document for self-worth, their dream for life frequently became positive.

Those who suffer addiction and other disorders may do so because they have lived with a lie, fostered on them by some sick person or some well-meaning soul. Even if it was a lie, they assumed it was the truth and acted as if it were. Their hope for recovery and transformation is to discover the truth. Truth establishes a firm foundation upon which we may build our positive dreams. Finding and following the truth are the keys that unlock the door to freedom for anyone who practices abuse.

Recognizing that, facilitators for rehabilitation have one more critical criterion with which to work. The centrality of truth in human health and wholeness underscores the urgency for all of us to seek it as a preventive against and a cure for negative dreams.

We must connect our dreams to what makes us feel good. Let us not confuse this with what makes us feel less bad. Even though they have something in common, they are not the same. The primary reason for abuse is it makes a person feel less bad at the moment.

Negative dreams, at best, make us feel less bad. Usually, they make no positive contribution. Negative dreams drive people who know no other way to find relief. For those who hurt, any relief is better than constant agony in the guts. For those who hurt and for those who are happy, positive dreams enable us to feel good deep inside by validating our own worth. I realize there is a problem with precise interpretation of "feel good" but at least it gives us a point at which to begin. It is not a promotion of, "If it feels good, do it." However, well-adjusted people do not search for things to do that make them feel bad.

They eventually cease to do things that have no positive pay back. Abusers continue to abuse because that is as close as they can get to "feeling good." Positive dreams enable us to feel good about who we are, our accomplishments, and enticing future possibilities for ourselves and others. Positive dreams relieve inner pain and pressure. A word of caution in order. Positive dreams are not chosen just to make us feel good. If that is the case, feeling good is our supreme concern, our "god." Feeling good comes as the result and reward of the dream, not as the primary reason for it. Therefore, there must be some higher standard by which dreams are properly judged. That standard, I propose, is "appropriate love."

Dr. Maxwell Maltz's book, entitled "Psycho-cybernetics" (Pocket Book, 1976), offers insight into the power of dreams. I am no scholar on the subject but it points to the importance of our self- image and the use of our mind. Two illustrations on the subject may help us. An ardent golfer sat quietly and envisioned, dreamed, of making a perfect golf swing. He practiced that perfect shot over and over in his mind. He significantly reduced his average score during his next round of golf.

A musician took a piece of sheet music she had not previously seen. She also sat practicing the music in her mind and envisioned, dreamed, of playing it perfectly. She later went to the appropriate musical instrument and flawlessly performed the piece of music.

Excessively simplified, Psycho-cybernetics includes practicing in our mind the perfect accomplishment of our dream.

The dreams we have while we are awake apparently fit neatly into this framework. It is as if our dreams etch tracks or grooves in our minds that subconsciously guide our behavior. Therefore, anyone whose mind is etched with the image of "I'm no damn good," almost automatically acts it out. They simply practice in their body what they have repeatedly pondered in their mind. Those who have a high self-image operate from a different etching in the mind. They know they have value and they act like it. Both types, I suspect, give little thought to what is going on in them and assume, "That's just the way it is."

Here is another clue for rehabilitation and transformation of those who suffer from low self-esteem. They desperately need encouragement and an opportunity to imagine, dream, what life could be if things were better for them. Counselors can play a game with clients called, "What might happen if" and the "ifs" are in the realm of recognized possibility for the person needing help. It is crucial for all abusers to picture in their mind, dream of, being clean, sober and free.

They need to practice in their mind how they will refuse the first offer of a hit of drugs, a drink of booze, or the temptation to abuse again. They need to repeatedly practice, practice, practice until it is indelibly etched in their brains. It is essential for them to envision a new way of dealing with old recurring problems that previously resulted in using drugs, drink, or other abusive behavior.

Anyone familiar with the recovery process knows these issues are sure to arise after a person returns to their previous habitat. Temptation will come from where it previously came and it will come at a person's weakest point. Having recognized that, it is mandatory for those seeking recovery to practice in their minds until they are sure how they want to respond and are comfortable with it.

One monumental difference between recidivism and recovery hinges on this matter. Too many people depart recovery programs totally unprepared to properly confront the coming temptations because there are no new "action tracks" etched in their mind.

Likewise, those who seek recovery through self-help programs and group work must be made aware of the need to seriously practice in their mind what they intend to do with their body. Even though somewhat diminished, old grooves and dreams are still there and will eventually dominate unless replaced by strong, well-defined new ones.

Motivation for recovery of any kind depends on a person's self-image and personal abilities. One's poor self-image must be improved before recovery is possible.

"Nothing happens unless first a dream." We must amend that quote by saying recovery does not happen unless a person is first able to dream positively. Several years ago, Dr. Norman Vincent Peale proclaimed "the power of positive thinking." Some wag suggested Dr. Peale needed to be repealed. Regardless of what we may thinkabout his beliefs, he is on target when he emphasizes the necessity to consciously envision and dream in order to get what we want.

Acquiring a Cadillac, remaining alcohol and drug free, or gaining freedom from any abusive behavior will require more than positive thoughts and dreams. However, unless and until we have positive thoughts and dreams, we will not get or seriously work to attain something better for ourselves. Unless we believe we can do it, we will never try. Here is another clue for those who seek to facilitate recovery.

Perhaps it is unwise, even foolish, to suggest some possible positive dreams for all of us but I am willing to take that risk. Regardless of what is suggested, some subjects will be omitted. These suggestions require personal adjustment, improvement and expansion to meet individual needs. The following suggestions are applicable for recovery from any addiction, abuse, deviant behavior, personal malady, etc.

All who desire recovery from any malady will be helped by a dream for strength to call their illnesses and hurts by their real name or else they eventually die in their misery. We gain some added control over our malady if we properly name it. As long as anyone refuses to admit they have a problem and name it, the likelihood of recovery is almost nil.

This addresses the subject of denial, a common practice among so many who have problems. Addicts and heavy abusers do not have a monopoly on denial. It is frequently practiced in minuscule or large amounts by most of us. It can be as simple as habitually refusing to honestly say what we think, how we feel or what we want. It includes always demanding our own way. It extends to the point of heavy addiction and a refusal to admit there is a problem.

From the perspective of those who practice it, denial is done for a reason. Denial will eventually destroy us or cause us to destroy ourselves. We cannot forever live happily and healthy in the land of make-believe. If we try, our carriage eventually turns into a pumpkin. The only cure for our malady is to first call it by its name and admit it belongs to us. We must honesty admit, "I have a drinking problem," or "I have a drug problem," or "I have a whatever-it-is problem,"

because nothing of lasting value will be done until we take that step. The "Twelve Steps" program of A. A. speaks eloquently on this point. Any denial left unchallenged may easily grow into a monster. Once again, we are reminded that truth and reality are the keys to wholeness. Recognizing and naming our malady may be painful but it is the only way we can move toward recovery at any level.

Most of us would profit by dreaming for an opportunity to review our history, to identify where or how we were injured and to remove the garbage so that healing and wholeness may come. This would be helpful for everyone who hurts but it is extremely important for heavy abusers and addicts. When given a chance, almost every one of them will give specific dates, places and events that convinced them they were worthless. Those specifics stand like neon signs constantly reminding them who they are. They are much more likely to recover if they can be taken emotionally and symbolically back beyond that point and given assistance to properly interpret and understand it as they move through it again.

Having "relived" that painful part of life under different conditions, they are more likely to break the barrier that previously prevented wholesome living. Mental institutions have used this approach with great success. Severely ill mental patients were symbolically brought through life's stages. Some were put in enlarged baby beds, wore diapers, etc. Special attention helped them quickly retrace their developmental history without getting hung or hurt at any point. They were offered new interpretations and explanations for major stumbling blocks. I understand the success rate with such programs is remarkable. If that works for them then it should and does work in slightly different settings, especially for abusers.

This approach has been employed with criminals and victims. A woman who had been raped was purposefully brought face to face with the rapist. They came to know something about each other's personal history. The rapist shared some of his painful history and genuinely apologized to her for what he had done. The face to face meeting did not negate the rape nor did it dissolve all the problems that followed. In some small measure, the two people connected at some point prior to the rape and in a new way. That connection diminished some of the pain associated with the crime and allowed them to move forward on a different level. These two people may continue to suffer for a long time but they may have taken the only step that makes renewal possible for either.

I have personally profited from carefully re-thinking my family history. My mother married when she was only a child herself. She gave birth to her first daughter before she was sixteen. By seventeen, she had a second daughter. A third was born when she was nineteen. Her next two children were boys, the next was a girl and the last was a boy, making a total of seven children. My mother had a favorite child and I was not it. At least some of the children knew who it was and occasionally spoke about it. I am the fifth child of the family and the favored child is the sixth, born about four years after me.

Within a few years of my younger sister's birth, I began to suspect favoritism toward her from our mother. By the time I reached my teens, I had no doubt. My mother searched for an excuse to chastise and paddle me. In many cases, it appeared my sister was involved in some way but I got the spanking. She broke an egg in the hen house while I was elsewhere but I was spanked. If she said I put my toe in a bucket of water and I said I did not, she was believed and I was spanked. There were numerous events where it was apparent to me that favoritism existed. It continued long after both she and I married and had our children. My early awareness of that favoritism affected my feelings toward, and possible treatment of, my mother and sister from my pre-teen years until long after I entered the military.

There is other evidence of favoritism. While on a remote military assignment, I received notice that my wife was seriously ill and I was immediately needed at home. I rushed home for her serious surgery. Her doctor advised me that she might not survive. Thankfully, she did survive. Three weeks later, I return to my military duty.

When I departed from my wife, she had no one to care for her. She could not drive and our two young children were in her care. My parents lived about forty miles away but did not come even once to check on her following my departure. My younger sister lived about the same distance in the opposite direction from them. During my wife's recovery, as well as other times, my parents often drove to my sister's house in order to hold the baby during her trip to the doctor. The stated reason was that the baby might be fretful after seeing the doctor. My father was well aware of this favoritism More than once he made a joking reference to having only two grandchildren, my sister's. He said people thought they had only those two, by the way he and Mom acted.

During a personal growth seminar sponsored by the Air Force, I had an opportunity to review my history and discover rough spots that needed repair. I focused on my mother's favoritism and my response to it. Through that process I found wonderful relief. I pondered the circumstances and conditions into which I was born.

My mother married at fifteen, just like her mother and some of her older sisters. She dropped out of school before finishing the eighth grade. Her first three children were girls. Three months after my mother turned twenty, the third girl, her baby at that time, died from a stomach disorder. My mother never admitted it but I firmly believe she blamed herself for the child's death.

Since her next two children were boys, my older brother and I, she welcomed our birth without any emotional upheaval, possibly because we were potential farm hands. When my younger sister was born, my mother immediately remembered her last girl child whom she lost. Consciously or subconsciously, she said, "I may have lost that one through some fault of my own but you can bet your last dollar I will do everything possible to keep from losing this one." From that day forward, my mom gave special attention to that child, even though another son was born six years later. Protection of that girl child took precedence over many other things in her life.

I symbolically returned to that earlier period of my life. After I pondered those events and circumstances, I came to a different understanding of my mother. She lacked formal education, married just after turning fifteen, was a mother at fifteen, birthed three children prior to twenty, lost a child in death just after turning twenty, labored long hours in the home and in the field as a farmer's wife, lacked modern conveniences and domestic help, etc. It is not strange that she might have minor emotional problems. I began wondering why she did not have more. I concluded my mother did exceptionally well with what she had and deserved a medal for what she accomplished.

My feelings toward her changed and I felt differently about my sister who deserves no blame for what my mother did. I came to that understanding only after I reviewed my history, identified the bump and repaired some personal damage. The process changed me and it has worked for many others. It is a remarkably helpful approach for those who are painfully hooked on some part of their history.

Those of us who hurt may profit from dreaming of a place where we can openly and honestly acknowledge our pain and where we may also experience appropriate love. Words fail to describe how wonderful it is to be in a place where you can admit what you feel or think without fear of reprisal. We are indeed fortunate to find a place where we can be ourselves, without pretense or posturing.

Great relief comes when we are free to show our warts and flaws to others and they do not scoff or scorn but rather affirm us for who we are and will gladly help if we ask. Dr. Carlyle Marney, a noted religious leader, called such a place his "House Church." It was composed of six or eight friends. Having found such a place, we know we are genuinely loved. It is amazing how therapeutic appropriate love is. It is also amazing what a person can endure when they know someone located somewhere truly loves them. We all long to know we are genuinely loved, not just by what people say but also by the way they act.

A lad complained that no one really loved him. A bystander encouraged him to cheer up and assured him that God loved him.

"Yes, I know," he said, "but right now I'd like to be loved by someone who has skin on them."

All of us understand that desire. We long for a place where we will be loved in spite of who and what we presently are. Judeo-Christian religion emphasizes God's love for all humanity, regardless of who we are or what we have done. We are prone to respond more favorably to God's love when it is expressed through someone with skin. The "Twelve Steps" program of A.A. beautifully combines these two thoughts. It speaks of commitment to a "Higher Power" and encourages genuine love from its participants so that others may maintain sobriety.

Knowing we are free to acknowledge our pain without jeopardizing love from others enables recovery and growth.

It may be helpful to dream of the day when remembering our previous weakness will also remind us of our present strengths and erase fears because we have survived, in spite of our malady. This dream may be more important to some than it is to others. It is especially important to those with major maladies and to those who have long endured them. I repeatedly and honestly complemented participants in treatment programs for their ability to endure. Many of them went through situations and experiences that I may not have survived.

Their fascinating and almost unbelievable tales of endurance and survival would make them heroes were they not addicts and abusers. I marveled at their ingenuity and I told them. Since they proved their ability to survive in their malady, I know they can survive without it. Clean and sober living has problems but they are not equal to what they previously endured.

Having recognized their noteworthy accomplishment in the past, having gained a modicum of self-worth, they are far more likely to believe they can survive a new lifestyle. Many of them were about as low as one can get and saw the worst there was to see but they survived. What was left to fear because they personally saw and survived the worst? Their previous weakness pointed out a special and present strength that can lead them to successful change. They need not fear because they know they have what it takes to survive.

During my childhood days on the farm, an elderly neighbor's doctor told him he must give up smoking tobacco. He smoked for years and was heavily addicted to it but was determined to quit. He developed an unusual approach to break his habit. He plowed with a can of tobacco in the bib pocket of his overalls. He worked until his craving to smoke almost exceeded his resistance.

At that point, he stopped his mule, sat on the plow handle, removed the can of tobacco from his pocket, opened it, stirred it with his finger, smelled it, looked at it and said, "I want to smoke you so bad I can hardly resist but I'm bigger than you."

He then closed the can, placed the tobacco in his pocket and plowed some more. He endured and survived the worst possible pains caused by withdrawal from nicotine. There was nothing else to fear from tobacco. He saw and endured the worst it could give. The same can be true for us as we overcome our maladies.

Our maladies may not be as detrimental as we originally thought. The human ability to recover is amazing and takes strange twists and turns. Through our maladies we may have learned some of life's most significant lessons. If we are fortunate enough to do that, or if we allow them to do that for us, we are empowered for the future. Maladies may teach us what we might not learn otherwise. It would be a mistake for us to think that once we have overcome a malady, we will never have another. However, those who previously overcame may have greater confidence and far less fear about the future. They have endured the worst and survived. They are driven by a new dream.

It may be wise for us to dream of the day when we will be reasonably satisfied with who and what we are, at least for the moment. How wonderful it would be if each of us could truthfully say, "It's okay to be me." So many of us are deeply dissatisfied with who and where we are in life. We are constantly implored to be what we are not and led to believe there is no possible peace for us where we are. That is a bunch of bull!

If happiness is ever found, it will be where we are. We will never find it where we aren't. It is available only where we are.

It cannot be piped in or transported from some other place. We find it where we are or we don't find it. If we are to find it where we are, we may have to alter our thoughts and behavior. If we desire change, we may not forever remain where we presently are but that is the only place to begin making improvements.

We must first fully accept what and who we are at this time and place. If we are an alcoholic, a drug user, an abuser of any sort, lazy, etc., we must admit it. It is OK to be what we are. No apologies, excuses or justifications are necessary. Who we are does not negate what we may later choose to do. Nothing productive can or will happen until we make peace with who we are. The truth of the matter is that we may never be able to completely change who we are. However, we can surely make adjustments that radically change what we do.

My parishioner at a country church perfectly illustrated the point of momentary satisfaction. His wife went on an errand from which she would not return until after dark. Before leaving, she asked him to milk the cow, so she would not need to upon her return.

When she returned home, she discovered the "un-milked" cow standing at the pasture gate calling for her calf. The husband war sitting on the front porch, strumming on his guitar, loudly singing, "I have a satisfied mind." This is an analogy for life. The call of unfinished chores reminds us that we still have things to do but there are times when we need to sit on life's porch with a satisfied mind, heart and spirit. The awareness and acceptance of what we are gives us authority to sit and sing. Positive dreams empower us to move when we are ready.

Dreams provide powerful motivations that are either positive or negative. Most of our actions are expressions of some dream. Negative dreams tend to become painful and unending nightmares. Positive dreams may not always be pain free but they alone enable us to move in that direction. They are keys to health, happiness and wholeness. There is great virtue and value in having only positive dreams. That too is an appropriate dream! Whatever our dreams, they constantly control us because we are always driven by a dream.

CHAPTER 12

Where to From Here?

Years ago, I became alarmed at the amount of time wasted by asking and answering inappropriate questions. As a counselor, therapist and friend I repeatedly encouraged others to ask and answer questions most appropriate to their specific situation. For that reason, I required patients under my tutelage in treatment centers to confront issues of great importance for their recovery. Many questions vital to them are also extremely important to all of us, especially when seeking recovery and renewal in any form.

One of those vital questions is, "Where to from here?" I first addressed that question to patients who anticipated imminent graduation from their treatment program. I designed it for two specific purposes. First, I wanted patients to become more aware of the veiled and teasing temptations to continue their old lifestyle. Second, I sought to facilitate gathering information and insights that would truly help them if they chose clean and sober living. Eventually, it dawned upon me that this question and its two original purposes have a much wider application. It is applicable for everyone at every crossroads in life. Every new beginning should start there. Each day might be radically different if we started with that question. The celebration of success could appropriately conclude with it. Having recognized our failure, is there a more appropriate question?

"Where to from here?" The question initially appears to have many possible answers. Regardless of the assumed options or amount of verbiage used to respond, there are two legitimate answers. They are vastly diverse and have very different results.

The first option is a continuation of the old lifestyle. It is amazing how many ways we can express that choice even when we thought we chose its opposite. It is easily disguised in many forms and hides behind what first appears practical and safe. It is the unknown choice of those who say they want to remain clean and sober but must wait and see what is "out there" before making definite plans on how to proceed.

The same result comes to those who say they will cease abusive behavior but delay any effort to mend their actions. Such answers may make some sense to those who give them because they do not know what they will find when they start over. Many of them previously created a gigantic mess and they do not know its status or outcome. They wonder how they can make definite commitments with so few known facts. They do not want to fail again so they move slowly and cautiously, only to be trapped by their indecisiveness. Those determined to "wait and see" seldom wait long before they see themselves in the old lifestyle, usually with no knowledge of why or how they got there.

Some say they want to be clean and sober, freed from abusive behavior, given a new chance in life, etc., but they must first ascertain what "significant others" want and think before making a definite plan.

Once again, those who depart treatment centers or attempt any recovery while harboring such thoughts are doomed to fail. It sounds good on the surface because it reflects family concerns and togetherness. Persons from dysfunctional families, broken relationships and frequent failures may feel the necessity to include others in their decision as proof of a new beginning. The primary flaw in such reasoning is that they have the immediate problem, not someone else. On the surface, such an answer may first sound reasonable but it is only another disguised way of saying they chose the old lifestyle. We previously spoke of the urgency for personal choices and the fate of those who cannot or will not make them.

"Where to from here?" There are those who respond to the question by denying its validity. They firmly deny the right of another to interfere in their life with an offer to help them decide where to go or how to get there. In essence, they proclaim self-sufficiency and thereby deny or belittle the present problem from which they suffer. If they are truly self-sufficient, we wonder why they find themselves in their present situation. They are the ones who sleep through class sessions during their treatment program, who refuse to attend A.A. or N.A. meetings, who never take a personal improvement course, and who refuse to visit a competent counselor. Recovery and renewal aren't really important to such people. It is impossible for them. The old lifestyle awaits them with open arms. Their personal "devils" have nothing to fear.

The old lifestyle may disguise itself in the promise of moderation. Someone may conclude, "If 'too much' is my problem I will practice moderation and all difficulties in that area will disappear." That approach disregards the power of addiction and deviant behavior. We cannot willfully master our addiction or ingrained behavior by moderation, even with extensive treatment.

Addiction is a demonic power that permeates us and seeks ultimate control. Once that "devil" gets his foot inside the door, he not only seeks to stay but he may call his kin to move in with him or in his place. If expelled, he way resides just outside the door.

Therefore, addiction and abnormal behavior of any type cannot be cured with moderation alone. Those who believe moderation is answer have opened the door to the old lifestyle.

The old lifestyle is easily renewed through these numerous other unsuspected ways. Regardless of enticing disguises and multitude of promises, the old lifestyle will continually be painful, even if one briefly flirted with possible change. Everyone who mistakenly or purposefully chooses the old lifestyle will reap its painful reward, even if tricked & trapped into it. "Where to from here?" By many different words and ways, we can answer, "Back to the old lifestyle." We ask again, "Where to from here?" The second possible answer, like the first, is expressed in various forms and verbiage. This multifaceted answer is best summarized with the word "recovery" or "renewal." Anything included in this answer must be synonymous with and supportive of that process. Called by whatever name, it is a new lifestyle we purposefully endeavor to enter

In our search for this second answer, we recognize the dangers of the old lifestyle and seek to replace it with something better. We begin with the full recognition of the foe's power and our personal weakness when fighting solo. Being aware that the demonic spirit within can overpower us through its trickery and lies, we openly confess our past weakness and our present need for help. Since we are always controlled by a "higher power," we must choose an ally and not an enemy. All new beginnings are treacherous, so we must continue with care and caution. Given all that, it is impossible for anyone to quickly delineate a precisely tailored plan for personal recovery.

Making a wise decision on where we go from here is not easy but it is possible. The second answer is always predicated on our recognition that we want and need recovery. That fact must never be forgotten or subjugated. Anyone entering recovery and renewal must cautiously seek whatever meets their specific need. In searching for our own answer, a wise person will carefully examine what others have found to be extremely helpful. For abusers of drugs and alcohol, there is nothing better than N.A. or A.A. There are other valid programs but none have the accessibility and success of these two in their specific area.

Anyone reluctant to try a proven program is reminded of the man who accompanied his lady friend on a picnic. Due to previous experiences, he was hesitant to eat the food she had prepared. After some time, he decided to try it because the millions of ants seeking it could not be all wrong. Likewise, the multitudes of people who received life-giving support from these well-known programs were not all wrong.

More and more specialty groups are forming to meet specific needs of those seeking recovery and renewal. They cover such subject as overeating, gambling, personality adjustments, behavior modification, etc. Where no needed specialty group exists, competent counselors are usually available and may help establish such groups. Finding a useful program and helpful people demands time and effort but it is essential for recovery. A group's answer is never our answer because no one can recover for another. We may borrow from others by tailoring their answer to fit us. No possible answer or selected program can enhance recovery and renewal unless or until the participant is genuinely committed to it. Finding our answer to where we go from here will take extensive time and energy but proper help is available.

Where to from here? Individual answers may be given in different forms and with diverse verbiage but every personal answer will eventually be included in one of the two categories mentioned above. Everyone standing on the threshold of a new beginning will successfully cross the threshold or return to the old lifestyle.

Regardless of how hard one may try, it is impossible to live for long with one foot on each side of the door. Regardless of how much we may wish for another person to take responsibility for our desired change or to identify a precise plan of attack, each person is responsible for himself or herself. Recovery and renewal can come no other way. I have been deeply affected by what we called, in my youth, "Negro Spirituals."

Their powerful words portray eternal truths. Words from one of those emphasize individual responsibility. I do not recall its exact words but they are similar to the following. "You got to walk that lonesome valley. You got to go there by yourself. There's no one here who can go there for you. You got to go there by yourself." We have often wished it were not so but most of life's major decisions are made in agonizing loneliness.

That truth underscores the urgency of adequate preparation and the necessity for a strong support group. Proper preparation and personal support help us make wise and necessary choices. They remove some of the agony associated with making lonely decisions. This principle was clearly illustrated by Jesus in a New Testament story. While in the Garden of Gethsemane, he had to choose possible death or renunciation of his ministry.

His closest disciples accompanied him to a particular point. Apparently, they had seriously discussed the issue before him. He probably asked what they thought and heard. After some discussion, Jesus instructed his closest disciples to wait while he withdrew in solitude to make the momentous decision. Whatever the answer to the question, it had to be his alone.

That is the nature of answering serious questions and making crucial decisions. Regardless of who they are, others can accompany us only to a point. Mary, Sue, John and Jim can make important contributions by sharing their ideas and insights about our situation. After that, each of us must decide. Each of us does decide, consciously or not. As the poster on my office wall proclaimed, "Not to decide is to decide."

Answering this major question, or making any other significant decision, is problematic for many, due to experience. In some cases, dominating parents did not allow their child to make big decisions or to practice with little ones. Making a major decision is unknown and unwelcome by persons from that type family. Recognizing their inexperience and inability, they are naturally prone to delay a decision.

Scarlet O'Hara, in "Gone With The Wind", was such a person because she repeatedly said, "I'll worry about that tomorrow." I repeatedly marvel at and profit from the wisdom of my formally uneducated father. He habitually allowed opportunities for me to make significant decisions. When I was a teenager, he sought my suggestions on things about which he must decide and he depended on my decision making. Consequently my future decision making is far less frightening or painful because I had an excellent teacher and some serious practice.

Others are reluctant to formulate definite answers and make decisions due to past mistakes that were personally painful or very costly. Their histories reflect their repeated failure. They do not want to fail again. On the basis of their track record, they conclude that making a major decision is the beginning of another failure and they do not want the accompanying pain. From their point of view, no decision is the best decision. In their effort to make no decision, they have made a gigantic one. Those who hold that point of view will never travel the road to recovery and renewal.

Deciding the answer for a specific question is denounced by some, due to the scathing ridicule and fierce scorn received following former decisions. Dominating parents, a strict boss, a forceful mate, a misinformed associate, etc., are possible sources of such scorn. Few of us appreciate ridicule and scorn from any source. We understand some of the problem faced by those in that situation. As sad as it is, their options are to tolerate any scorn fostered by a new beginning or endure the pain of their old lifestyle. Either approach will have its pains and problems but only the former leads to recovery and renewal.

Having emphasized the individual and agonizing process of answering personal questions and making major decisions, we must quickly add that competent help is available and appropriate, both before and after the process. A wise person will ask for help in difficult times because asking is a sign of strength, not weakness.

Males generally have difficulty accepting the wisdom of asking for help. Imagine the hours that could have been saved and the anger that could have been avoided if only the male driver had stopped and asked for directions. The same can be said about life in general. We can only surmise the amount of personal misery, loss and waste of time that came to anyone who could not or would not ask for suggestions from those who knew the route. Every person who needs help can surely find it in today's society.

However, we are not compelled to accept every offer of help that comes to us. Certain people offer help for their good and not ours. Inadequate helpers deserve no opportunity to help. We fortunately have a multitude of competent helpers with whom we can honestly and safely discuss our innermost problems about which we must decide. Refusing to use competent helpers, both before and after making a major decision, hobbles us. Recovery and renewal are extremely difficult, if not impossible, when attempted alone. Our need for others during recovery and renewal is easily illustrated. The next time you barbecue, isolate a glowing briquette and observe how quickly it loses its heat. Isolated recovery and renewal most often meet similar results. We will soon lose our heat. Solo recovery is as promising as keeping an isolated charcoal hot.

Competent help and genuine support are usually available but we must look for them in the proper place and under the proper conditions. A young man discussed with his dad the difficulty of finding "nice" girls to date. The son said, "Dad, you just don't understand how it is. Girls with the character and qualities of Mom are hard to find."

The conversation continued and the father shared his wisdom by saying, "Son, let me ask you a question. If you decided to dig for diamonds, would you first look for them in the city sewer?" The son instantly got the message and replied, "Dad, please don't say another word about that subject." He knew that his dad knew some of the places he had looked. Competent and caring helpers, like diamonds, are available but there are certain places where they are more likely to be found.

Where to from here? If we are serious about recovery, renewal and personal growth, we must go through a three-pronged process. That process is more mental than emotional but both are involved. Emotions are acutely essential and this does not negate prior comments about them.

The first facet of the required process is developing a personal attitude. Specifically, the attitude affirms it is OK to be me. I have repeatedly discovered people who were ashamed of being themselves. I get perturbed when teachers ask their students, "Who would you like to be?"

The question conveys the idea that the child should not be who they are. Injury is added to insult when a teacher punishes the child who said, "I just want to be me." Parents, teachers and other well-meaning people easily convey that something is wrong with a child by saying, "Why can't you be like your sister?" "I wish your hair were not straight." "Why are you so dense?" "You are no good."

Having repeatedly heard such comments, the child naturally concludes it has a flaw and wishes it was someone else. We should not be surprised to learn that, in time, they try to be somebody else by using drugs, alcohol, sexual abuse, excessive eating, generally misbehaving, etc. Their use and abuse come primarily from a painful dissatisfaction with how they see themselves. As far as they are concerned, "It is not okay to be me." There are numerous ways by which we can convey our wish to be someone other than who we are.

I do not know who you wish to be but I can tell you who you are. You are you! Regardless of our wishing and pretending, at any given moment we are who we are! Popeye expressed a universal truth when he proclaimed, "I am what I am and that's all I am."

That is what I mean by attitude, the acceptance of the fact that I am what I am and that is presently all I am. At another point I emphasized the necessity to accept the attitude that it is OK to be me. That emphasis is applicable here and is worth repeating. This point is a gigantic stumbling block for those who hurt and for many who offer help. It is perfectly permissible to be a person who presently has problems with drugs, alcohol, abuse of any sort, behavior disorder, etc. It may be unhealthy and unwise but it is permissible to be there. Unless we accept that fact, there will be no foundation for renewal and no reason to attempt it.

Continued condemnation of ourselves destroys us but acceptance opens the door to renewal. A multitude of diverse situations and circumstances, many of which were far beyond my control, help explain and understand how I became who I am. I need to accept that fact without condemning others or myself. If the truth is told, I did exceptionally well with the opportunities I had. I should receive a commendation for my successes instead of condemnation for my failures. "What do you know! It is OK. to be me!" This positive attitude provides mental and emotional impetus to wisely answer where we go from here. Otherwise, we cannot get there from here!

The second facet of this necessary approach to recovery and renewal is a firm belief that recovery is possible for me. Before I decide where to go from here, I must truthfully believe "I can get there from here" or "I can do it." Without that belief, no one will ever make a serious attempt to begin the journey.

One who firmly believes they will eventually fail cannot make a serious attempt to begin the process nor will they allow themselvesto succeed if they make an effort. Those who never expect to win cannot and will not become fully engaged in the grueling game.

The belief that "I am no good" must be replaced with the belief that "recovery is possible for me" or recovery will fail. Failure to recognize this fact created a major stumbling block in many programs offered in treatment centers and elsewhere. Numerous patients graduated from the program long before they reached the conviction that recovery was possible for them.

Without that belief, recidivism was almost guaranteed. Pleas and encouragement for recovery that are based on health, finance, family, religion, reason, etc., will fail unless the patient first believes recovery is personally possible. All information on how recovery can be accomplished is premature and possibly wasted until the person believes they can do it.

I often remember a childhood parable about a little train engine. On a cold and snowy night, all except one of the big engines were safely gathered in the roundhouse. Word came that the absent engine was stalled on the other side of a mountain and desperately needed help to return with its cargo.

One after the other, each big engine was asked to render assistance. Each gave their own excuse and they all declined. There was only one remaining engine but he was very small. If the large engines thought it was too dangerous for them why should anyone ask him to go? He was the last hope and he was asked to assist. Without hesitation, he agreed to do his best. Out into the blizzard he chugged, singing as he went, "I think I can. I think I can."

He found the other engine, hitched to it, and slowly began to climb the slippery mountain. With wheels spinning and a load he could not be expected to pull alone, he continued to slowly sing, "I think I can. I think I can." Persistence and conviction enabled the

two trains to climb the mountain. When success became obvious, the little engine began to sing a little faster, "I thought I could. I thought I could." As the two trains headed home down the mountain, the little engine sang faster and faster, "I knew I could. I knew I could. I knew I could."

People, like the little engine, must "think I can" or we refuse to try.

As long as we "think we can," we will endure slow progress and very unpleasant conditions. At this point in recovery, we profit from all available help and encouragement. Strong support from those who understand us is critical. Personal testimonies from s uccessful travelers enable us to maintain our belief that we can win too. Once captivated by this conviction, we are ready for the next step.

The third prong of the recovery process is called commitment. If I have a wholesome attitude about myself and a belief that I can do it, I need to add a genuine commitment to carefully find and closely follow the road to recovery and renewal.

Once I definitely decide I want recovery, there must be no residue of doubt or a "maybe yes, maybe no" approach. At this point, I need a definite goal and a rough outline of how I might get there. As strange as it may first sound, I do not initially need a precise map for every step of the journey.

Such a map is impractical and impossible. It is impossible to have advance knowledge of every possible step or choice on the journey but it is necessary that I make a commitment to take whatever step seems most appropriate at the time. I first need a firm commitment to reach the goal by following the best route for me. As with any journey, this one must be carefully planned by using all available data but designed to allow for adjustments in light of new information and circumstances.

Secondary commitments make it easier to keep the primary one. Those who have little experience with making firm commitments or having firm commitments made toward them will have difficulty understanding and making firm commitments at any level. Therefore, dividing the major commitment into smaller pieces may be less frightening than constantly confronting the larger one in its entirety.

There must be a commitment to cease certain things. If I have an alcohol or drug problem, a commitment to abstain is necessary. If I abuse my body or another person's body, a commitment to cease such behavior is required. Whatever the old malady may be, a commitment to deal with old problems in new and more productive ways is essential. A firm commitment to participate in proven programs for a specific problem makes practical sense. A commitment to seek competent help and support is advisable.

We must heed the call for a commitment that prevents the weaknesses of others from becoming stronger than our strengths. Others will use their weakness in an attempt drive us back to the old lifestyle because a change in us gives them a problem or makes their own problem more painful. Given who some of them are, their pleas may be enticing unless we maintain our basic commitment to pursue renewal.

An important and revealing commitment is to change the way we spend our time, money, and energy. The old lifestyle demanded so much from us in these areas. Numerous days, dollars, and degrading acts were wasted to justify our malady and behavior. We can no longer tolerate such waste and deceit because we are committed to something far more productive, namely a plan that moves us toward health, happiness and wholeness.

A commitment to health, happiness and wholeness is somewhat vague but may provide a basic skeleton that can be fleshed out with time and practice. That commitment gives us a guideline to govern behavior when nothing more precise is available. Similar comments can be made about the commitment to personal responsibility and growth. Each and all of these lesser commitments may be a beacon light that flashes periodic guidance when darkness seeks to impede our knowledge of where to go.

I will suggest one additional commitment but others may come to mind. It is a commitment to share with others who suffer what helped put me on the road to recovery. If recovery is to continue, I must be willing to help others. It is only in freely giving to others that we are able to maintain a life-giving portion for ourselves.

Our earlier comments about loving our neighbor as we love ourselves are directly related to this issue. Even as the glowing charcoal maintains its fire only if it shares it with others, so is it with all seriously seeking recovery. We must also remain in close contact with our kin. This is another area of our life where we can keep only what we give away. Given that fact, there should be no lack of commitment and no hesitation to participate in special groups designed for specific maladies.

Likewise, there should be no question of why those who successfully continue on the road to recovery have given so much of themselves to others on the journey. We draw strength from those near us and then we gladly share what we have received with any in need so that they and we may be empowered for the journey. Two broken sticks that are leaning against each other may prevent both from falling to the ground. The same can be said about us.

Where to from here? All who successfully recover go through this three-step process. There are no short cuts or bypasses. We must have the "Attitude" that we are OK, a basic "Belief" in our ability and a firm "Commitment" to do whatever is necessary for a successful journey. There are the "ABCs" of recovery and renewal.

The acrostics can be prominently posted on the bath room mirror, the dashboard of the car, in the office, etc., as a gentle reminder of the process in which we are engaged and as a rough road map for where we plan to go. These three letters begin the alphabet but they do not complete it. Likewise, attitude, belief and commitment only start us toward recovery but without a beginning there can be no successful conclusion.

Where to from here?
When first asked, that seemed to be a rather simple question. Having traced some of its multifaceted applications and ramifications, it is definitely not simple. If you were surprised by the question's

extensive ramification, fasten your seat belt because there is another dynamic dimension we have not addressed.

An additional dimension lurked in the shadows throughout much of the previous material but it has not made itself fully known. If I provided new insights into the cause, treatment and prevention of addiction, abusive behavior, maladjusted personality, etc., this fundamental question must be addressed not only to individuals but also to the society that produced them.

Society at large must also ask, "Where to from here?" I am aware

that society has no mind of its own. It is composed of individuals but often reflects a herd mentality. It may be somewhat different to address this question to society but the difference does not negate the necessity for extending the question.

Another, and perhaps lengthier, book is required to adequately probe the implications of addressing this question to the society in which we live. Our underlying expectation of society is to help alleviate human misery and promote health and wholeness. We want it guided by appropriate love. If it were guided exclusively by those fundamental concerns, we are incapable of comprehending the multitudinous changes that would occur in our social, political, economic, and educational systems. Congressional members would act differently and laws would be enacted through a different format and for a different purpose. Industry and businesses would operate from a new perspective.

If most human maladies have an underlying and identifiable cause, many of those causes are created and perpetuated by our society. All who honestly desire renewal for others and themselves are frequently confronted by social conditions that thwart the recovery process and encourage abuse. Even though each individual is responsible for his or her choices, modern society increasingly makes it almost impossible for an individual to choose freely.

As individuals, we are often herded, hounded and held by some segment of society. Modern trends and conditions indicate a new urgency for our social systems to seriously consider where they want to go from here. When our society becomes "a house divided against itself," similar to individuals, it too will eventually suffer and fail.

Some higher concern or principle affects our choices. We naturally ponder what society's ultimate guide will be. In short, what or who is its "god?" From a Judeo-Christian perspective, there is only one valid supreme power and that is God. If that phraseology frightens anyone, we may speak in more human terms.

"Appropriate love," described and defined elsewhere, is worthy of becoming our goal and guide. Anything less, for individuals or society, diminishes and disregards the human core and prevents health, happiness and wholeness for all. "Appropriate love" may be somewhat vague but it provides a valid guide for individuals or society to decide where we go from here. If individuals and society can effect a beginning that is motivated by "appropriate love," human suffering will be radically reduced and recovery will become commonplace.

Where to from here? The question initially sounded quite simple. After further consideration, we discovered its inescapable importance for every person and society. Whoever and wherever we are, each of us consciously and subconsciously answered that question more often than we previously realized.

We will continually answer it. It confronts us almost every moment we are awake and it disturbs our sleep. It is applicable when we experience pain in our gut, when we discover ways to make it disappear, when we are exceedingly happy, etc. It hovers over every pending personal and public decision.

Each individual and society must answer it at every available option. Having firmly and faithfully answered it at a specific time and place, it will not go away. It instantaneously becomes applicable at the next choice and we renew the decision-making process. There is no escape from it in this life. Perhaps that is how it should be. After all, recovery and renewal will commence and continue only if we consciously ask and constantly answer, "Where to from here?" This is another way to diminish and prevent "A Pain In The Gut."

ABOUT THE AUTHOR

Joseph C. Way was raised on a small farm in rural Mississippi and graduated from Georgetown High School. In 1956, he received his BA degree from Millsaps College in Jackson, Mississippi with a major in religion.

In 1960, he received a Master of Divinity Degree from Vanderbilt Divinity School, returned to Mississippi, was ordained an Elder, and assigned a pastorate. He joined the struggle to end segregation when he and twenty-seven other Methodist ministers signed a declaration of conscience. As a result, church officials denied him a pastoral appointment, forcing him to leave the state for employment and protection of his family. He is listed in Who's Who in American Methodism for contributions toward desegregation in Mississippi.

In 1964, he entered the Air Force as a chaplain and served for almost twenty-three years, retiring as a Lieutenant Colonel. Much of his military career was spent in counseling. At several assignments, he was a team member who prescribed and directed the regimen for military personnel identified with an alcohol or drug problem. He became a certified counselor for alcoholism and traveled widely to introduce a new approach to treatment and recovery.

In 1987, he retired from the Air Force and became the chaplain for a VA alcohol and drug treatment center. For the next five years, he refined his approach to treatment. The favorable response of the patients became the catalyst for writing this book.

Due to a shortage of Methodist ministers in the area, he was asked to pastor a prominent church. After five more years as a pastor, he retired again and moved to Georgetown, Texas where he lives with his wife

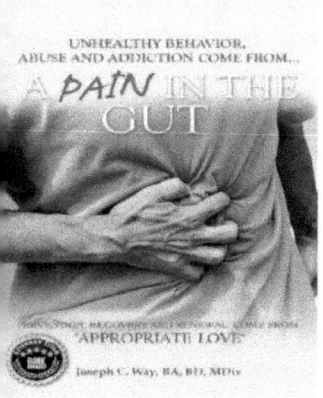

Hollywood Review

by Allison Walker

A Pain the Gut is about the ways everyone, universally, engages in addictive and unhealthy behaviors; not about colonoscopies, as you might have been thinking. AuthorJoseph C. Way maintains we all sometimes have a pain in our gut which we are seeking to ease. We may choose to ease this gut feeling with alcoholism, or seeing the negative in every situation, or being inflexible in our routines. The presence or absence of this gut feeling drives our self-destructive or self-affirming behaviors. In his book, *A Pain in the Gut*, Joseph C. Way shares his observations and experience earned over more than forty years as a chaplain, pastor, counselor and therapist specializing in drug and alcohol treatment.

When it comes to better understanding people suffering from addiction, Way's book does more to create empathy than any childhood tear-jerker story. Reading A Pain in the Gut, you come to understand the ways in your own life you sought to ease that pain in your gut, how you allowed yourself to become addicted to unhealthy habits, why you tried to find materialistic comforts to ease emotional discomfort. As Way says and readers will come to understand, "Their struggle was my struggle."

The US Review of Books

by Michelle Jacobs

Even though imperfect, this model helps us better understand human behavior. It is simple enough to easily understand but unique enough to inform and refresh."

With clarity and compassion, Way is a voice of support and hope in the midst of a personal crisis, which often manifests as physical pain in the body. So often, people want to numb the pain with drugs and alcohol, but this only exacerbates the despair. Instead, Way offers true balm for the pain with a model that helps people discover the causes of their addiction, which is the beginning of healing.

Literary Titan

I enjoyed how the author uses models to illustrate the link between unhealthy behaviors and addiction,to make the process simple and easy to understand. The writing flows in a smooth, informative style,which makes it easy to follow, with real-life and hypothetical instances that readers can relate to personally. Joseph C. Way narrates the story from his perspective, which makes it credible, as he has worked forty years as a pastor, therapist, and counselor. He includes numerous examples and anecdotal stories from patients, addicts, and others dealing with various situations.

A Pain in the Gut by Joseph C. Way is a compelling read, and I highly recommend it to anyone struggling with unhealthy behaviors or addictions. It's a refreshing read that helps individuals tackle challenges in life by offering quick, effective ways to manage the pain in the gut.

www.ingramcontent.com/pod-product-compliance
Lightning Source LLC
Chambersburg PA
CBHW051521120626
46551CB00012B/1025